MARY MOODY has been a prolific gardening author and a former presenter on ABC-TV's *Gardening Australia*. Her books include *The Good Life* (1981), *Au Revoir* (2001), *Last Tango in Toulouse* (2003) and *The Long Hot Summer* (2005). Mary divides her year between her farm near Bathurst in New South Wales and her house in south-west France.

Also by Mary Moody

Au Revoir
Last Tango in Toulouse
The Long Hot Summer

Lunch with Madame Murat

sweet surrender

sweet surrender

Love, Life and the Whole Damn Thing

Mary Moody

MACMILLAN
Pan Macmillan Australia

First published 2009 in Macmillan by Pan Macmillan Australia Pty Limited
1 Market Street, Sydney
Copyright © Mary Moody 2009

National Library of Australia
Cataloguing-in-Publication data:

Moody, Mary, 1950–
Sweet Surrender / Mary Moody.

9781405038355 (pbk.)

Moody, Mary, 1950– – Family.
Aging – Philosophy.

306.87092

Typeset in 11.5/16 pt New Baskerville by Midland Typesetters, Australia
Printed by McPherson's Printing Group

To Margaret and Ken

FOREWORD

This is the book I was never going to write. After the turbulent publication of *The Long Hot Summer* I was determined not to pen another memoir about the trials and tribulations of a certain middle-aged woman who happens to be me. During the book's marketing campaign and the author tour that accompanied it, I repeatedly declared that it would be the very last in the series. Inevitably, at every event where readers came to buy books for me to sign, they would ask, 'Will there be another book?' My emphatic 'no' seemed to cause dismay.

I tried to stick to my resolve. I worked on a daytime television program and a national evening radio show. I wrote a book about a restaurant that I love in France, and made a documentary about it. I followed that by writing and publishing an illustrated family cookbook. I was kept busy, as I had been for several years, leading Australians on treks in the Himalayas, and conducting walking tours through villages in south-west France. I spent months at a time with my ailing sister in Canada, and made the most of opportunities to be with my grandchildren, now scattered far and wide.

Then I attempted to write a book about my generation of women, the baby boomers, and how they were coping with ageing. I failed miserably. The analytical approach I had adopted seemed to me to lack real impact. At the end of the day, I decided, there's nothing more powerful than a personal story, told from the heart.

So here I am again, describing the vicissitudes of my life in these last four years. It's a painful and exhausting process writing such personal stories, yet also strangely cathartic and, in the end, satisfying. We all deal with the hiccups in our lives in different ways. I seem to deal with them by writing them down. Getting them onto paper always helps me come to terms with whatever it is that may be troubling me. Eventually, of course, I'll run out of subject matter, but in the meantime I'll just continue to live, and hopefully love, this strange journey called life.

Mary Moody
Yetholme, near Bathurst
December 2008

1

Among the many friends I've accumulated since my school days, only a few are still in their original unions. Several have been married and divorced more than once, and many now live alone, some more happily than others. Their experiences are no doubt a reflection of the wider community. More than forty percent of marriages end in divorce; second marriages are even more likely to finish that way.

My friends' marriages have ended for all the typical reasons. Sexual incompatibility, disputes about parenting styles and values, infidelity, drug and/or alcohol abuse, domestic violence, workaholism, financial troubles, and just plain 'falling out of love'. The children of these broken unions seem to have survived into adulthood with no more than the usual problems, and in my circle there is a generally accepting attitude towards the whole business of divorce. It happens, get on with it.

People are often surprised to discover that I am still with my husband, David – and not just because they've read my memoirs, and know that I ran away to France when I was in my early fifties and that the saga of my subsequent infidelities was played out in the public arena. No, it's the fact of our thirty-seven years of being together that shocks them, especially given the difference in our ages and characters. Within the space of one generation, the situation appears to have reversed. Divorce seems a more likely outcome than a ruby wedding anniversary, especially if a marriage has encountered rocky periods.

But what marriage doesn't encounter rocky periods? I know of no relationship that hasn't been through dismal patches. At some stage, most of my friends have considered separation or divorce. Indeed I have several friends, claiming to be happily married, who laughingly confess that if they owned a handgun they would have cheerfully taken aim at their partner on more than one occasion. As individuals we change so much over the years that it's not realistic to expect we will relate to a partner the same way in our fifties as we did in our twenties. Thank heavens for that.

What interests me at this stage of my life is not so much why people separate and divorce, but why they stay together. Why some relationships endure against the odds and others, which on the surface may have appeared to be perfect partnerships, fall by the way-side. People remain in long-term marriages for all sorts of reasons. There's a certain comfort and security in a relationship that has lasted twenty years or more. Your partnership becomes like an old pair of slippers, familiar, homely and reassuring. You don't have to make an effort to keep up a conversation, to impress or to find favour. You can be bad-tempered, irrational or hungover, and your partner will either take it in their stride or just ignore you. More than likely your partner has seen you give birth, throw up, fall on your bum, shake with rage, cry like a baby and scream like a banshee. You can burn the dinner, reverse the car into a wall, donate a large sum of money to charity without consultation, and your mate will probably accept that this is just part of the rich tapestry of living under the same roof as you.

Sexually, a long-term partner can be many things. Comfortable and familiar, then surprisingly passionate and spontaneous. Some long-term relationships allow sex to vanish altogether without it being a worry to either partner (this would not work for me); but most, I suspect, allow their sexuality to ebb and flow according to life circumstances. I find there is nothing like a few weeks or months of separation to awaken my desire for sex!

Sharing the marital bed is a very cosy arrangement. Even if there's not a lot of sex going on, the closeness of another human body is to my mind reassuring and soothing. When David is away from home I often half-wake in the middle of the night and put my arm out to him – then feel disappointed when I remember he isn't there.

Fear of being alone is undoubtedly one of the main reasons why couples remain together even when their relationship is less than perfect. Strong attachments to extended family and to mutual friends can make the thought of separation and divorce unbearable. People who have been close to you both for decades perceive you as a couple, and even though it's unlikely you will lose their friendship if you are no longer married, you know that somehow the relationship will change. And change, for many, is frightening. I know the thoughts that went through my mind when David and I came close to parting after more than thirty years. Frankly, I was terrified.

I remember having lunch with a very dear friend who had known us since the genesis of our relationship, and I felt an overwhelming sense of sadness that it would never be quite the same again if David and I split. My bond with my children, their partners and my grandchildren also played an important part in my final decision to remain in the relationship. I felt that somehow my marriage to David symbolised the family unit; as the patriarch and matriarch living in the comfortable old family home we were at the very core, the very heart of the family. I know this is a surprisingly conservative, old-fashioned notion, especially for someone who thinks of herself as anti-conservative. It startles me that I felt this so deeply, because I have never cared greatly about the institution of marriage – indeed David and I lived together for more than twenty years before we wed, and all our children were born during our de facto years.

I can only conclude that I have always felt a deep and abiding attachment to the whole notion of family – no doubt as a reaction to my turbulent childhood. There is an element of romanticism in this. As a young woman I nurtured a burning desire to create a perfect family to compensate for the fact that my childhood was troubled. I clung to this notion all my adult life and when it came to the crunch – to the point of separation – I simply couldn't let go of that attachment. Of course, there are no perfect families, so this ideal was a nonsense, yet it was a major consideration when I was facing the possibility of losing my marriage. My sense at the time was that if *we* were no longer together then the family was no longer a solid unit and I would have somehow failed in my resolve.

Failure: that's the crux of the matter. The expression *failed marriage* is no longer in common use but its underlying connotation remains. If your marriage doesn't endure then you have somehow failed: that's the perception. I am an independent and adventurous woman who enjoys living alone in France for part of each year. So fear of failing in my marriage feels like a contradiction. But the fact is that both aspects of my self are authentic. I don't want my marriage to fail, or my family to fall apart, but like many other women in their fifties, I need to live my life on my own terms.

This book is about doing that *without* trying to escape from married life. It's about finding meaning in the good things: work and family, food and wine, travel and meeting new people. It's about living through the troubles which occasionally assail us and our loved ones at certain stages of our lives. It's about facing the inevitability of the ageing process and, ultimately, death. About negotiating new relationships with adult children and letting go of attachments and unrealistic expectations. It's also about gaining some insight into who I am at this age and stage of my life, based on my myriad experiences along the way and, importantly, it is about understanding where I came from in the first place. And about accepting how that has profoundly impacted my decisions, even though my life has been very different to my mother's.

She was born in Sydney in the early hours of April Fool's Day, 1920. It was a homebirth, even though my grandmother was well into her forties and not in particularly good health. I was born on the day the Korean War broke out in June 1950. A large, healthy post-war baby.

My mother Muriel's generation survived the Great Depression and then World War II, and Muriel became a war bride on a ship to America. Not in the usual sense, since my father, Theo Moody, saw no military action and his equipment was a notebook and pencil: he was an Australian foreign correspondent in Washington and New York, and covered the war for the Sydney *Daily Telegraph* from the fireside press conferences of President Franklin D Roosevelt.

My childhood was an era of optimism and prosperity. There was plenty of food on the table and as a generation we enjoyed a sense of security and identity not experienced by our parents. We children of the fifties were generally well loved and well educated and this was the basis of our feelings of self confidence; our assurance of our place in the world. We were baby boomers, after all.

As a young woman my mother was a great beauty, but over the years her pride in her appearance seemed to slip. The sixties rolled around, and then the seventies. Muriel, by now aged in her fifties, allowed her raven hair to go grey. She stopped wearing make-up and swapped her smart working clothes for casual slacks and hand-knitted jumpers. She relaxed. Let go. Surrendered to the process of growing old without putting up a fight.

With hindsight, I believe she threw away her youth long before it was necessary. That typified her generation. She grew up in an era when the term 'teenager' hadn't even been coined. Girls of her age went from wearing short socks and court shoes to stockings and high heels overnight. The leap from childhood to womanhood was arbitrary and instantaneous.

At the other end of her life the same rule seemed to apply. She went from a well-groomed businesswoman to a greying grandmother in the blink of an eye.

It wasn't going to happen to me.

2

I've been fortunate in my career. As a school leaver I didn't give it much thought. My parents were both journalists, and I had grown up during a time when finding exactly the job you wanted was much easier and less competitive than it is today. I didn't go to university – degrees in communications hadn't been invented in the 1960s – I simply started work as a magazine copygirl, making tea and running messages at the *Australian Women's Weekly*. Before too long I was awarded a cadetship, a three-year on-the-job apprenticeship, and graduated as a graded journalist before I was twenty.

My career path has zigzagged according to my passions. As a young woman I loved film and television and was excited to work as a feature writer and reporter in those areas for several years. I started a family and was a passionate homemaker, then worked part time as a journalist on *House and Garden* magazine writing stories on domestic themes, before moving the family to Leura in the Blue Mountains. There I became a committed organic gardener and my work changed accordingly. For more than two decades, I wrote articles and edited books and magazines about the joys of gardening. I was keenly interested in health and alternative medicine, and in my thirties landed a job editing a national preventive health magazine. I was always keen on politics and environmental issues in local government and edited and co-published two anti-development local newspapers in the community where we lived.

In my early forties I was approached by ABC-TV to work on *Gardening Australia*, and thus began a very happy and productive nine years of my life. It was one of my busiest periods as I also juggled caring for four teenage children and my elderly mother, maintaining a large garden (partly for professional reasons), and meeting various other writing and editing commitments.

Since I became a graded journalist I have never gone looking for employment; whether because of my enthusiasm or my positive outlook on life, opportunities have always come my way and, although I sometimes felt daunted, I have been brave enough – or foolhardy enough – to seize them.

One of the crazier jobs I've had in recent years was being cast by the Nine Network as one of a panel of women for a daytime, live-to-air chat show. In late 2004, some time after my first two books were published, I was approached by an executive producer from the Nine Network and asked to audition for a program tentatively named *The Watercooler*. She was cagey about the format, which was based loosely on a successful, long-running American program *The View*.

I was flattered. For an older woman – I was fifty-four when the producer from Nine approached me – there are very few opportunities in the cut-throat world of television. The ABC is an exception to some extent, with women such as Geraldine Doogue and Caroline Jones still gracing the screen, but women over fifty seldom play prominent roles in commercial TV these days – I suppose the stand-out is Kerri-Anne Kennerley, who has been on screen for so long that nobody cares about her age.

The auditions were gruelling. I'm a journalist, not an actress, and was therefore unaccustomed to a process that can be soul-destroying for those who do not make it from one round to the next. Years before I had done an audition for *Gardening Australia*. Compared with this meat market, that earlier test was a doddle; a small crew (producer, cameraman and sound recordist) came to our house at Leura, and in ten minutes we shot a relaxed sample of me chatting away about various aspects of my much-loved garden. I got the job!

The Channel 9 test was different. There would be other women involved and we were to voice our opinions on various topics, from the news of the day to issues affecting young mothers at home. I felt quite comfortable with this. The chance to express my opinions and attitudes about the problems facing modern society was an opportunity I certainly didn't want to miss.

I must admit that when I quit *Gardening Australia* I was relaxed about not being tied to a weekly television commitment, and not the slightest bit fazed by the notion that I would probably never work in television again. In fact I felt relieved to be out of the thick of it. Yet here I was just a few years later, preparing to try out for a show that involved a daily commitment that would mean that I would have to live in Sydney for most of the week – madness! What I hadn't realised was that dozens of prospects were being tested out for the show on that particular day. When I arrived there were women in small groups chatting and comparing notes: I didn't know any of them and felt rather out of place and overwhelmed. I was dressed very simply in a linen suit – not power dressing but not casual either – and I had spent quite a bit of time getting my hair and make-up right because I had been told our auditions would be taped so that our performances could be seen by network executives.

Eventually it was my turn to face the camera alongside three other women to whom I had been introduced only minutes before. I was the oldest, by quite a margin, and everyone – not just me – seemed nervous and unsure of what was expected. We had been given a list of topics to think about – nothing very challenging – and the idea was that we were to bounce them around in a conversational manner, just as women would do when gathered around the watercooler or coffee-maker at the office. To be quite honest, I can't remember who the other women in that audition were, or what topics we bandied about. I do remember that after a rather shaky start I relaxed and had some fun – I tried to be as natural as possible and even managed to slip in a couple of slightly saucy one-liners. The experience wasn't as painful as I had feared.

When I heard nothing back from the network within several weeks, I assumed that I had been eliminated from the search. I had learned that more than sixty women from all around the country had been called in to the first round of auditions and I expected my chances of getting to the next stage of the process were very slim.

Then, out of the blue, I had a call-back from the producer. Could I come down for another round of screen tests? I was surprised but quite chuffed and wondered who else had been selected and what form the next audition would take. The producer told me the reaction around the network to my first tape was that I was knowledgeable and down to earth, yet wicked – an ingredient they wanted in the production.

This time a decision had been made to allow a 'getting to know you' session before the taping. I was introduced to three prospective co-hosts: the gorgeous ABC and SBS television journalist Indira Naidoo (I was a huge fan); another ABC journalist who I wasn't so familiar with, Shelley Horton; and tall, willowy, utterly beautiful Cleo Glyde, a former model who had become a magazine style editor. The four of us seemed to gel pretty quickly, chatting excitedly about the possibility of doing the program, and I was surprised to discover they had 'googled' me to discover my background. I hadn't even heard of Google in those days, and felt a bit underprepared; I had been living out of the city for years, and was no longer up on all the latest trends and technology. Cleo also talked about having a 'spray tan' so she would look better on camera. I'd never heard of a spray tan, so again I felt slightly naïve and not as savvy as the others.

It was obvious from the start that we had been cast to cover a range of requirements. Shelley was smart, funny and plump, a single woman in her late thirties without children. Indira was highly educated, intelligent and calm, also in her thirties, married but without children, and representing the 'ethnic' audience. Cleo was the glamour queen, clever and quick and doing it tough as a single mother. I was the token older woman, a mother and grandmother able to speak from life experience.

This time the audition was in a large studio with a mock-up set, and the highly experienced Liz Hayes was our moderator, steering us from one topic to the next. We did the best we could under the circumstances. The idea was to keep the conversation bouncing along quickly; to agree to disagree, and not to talk over the top of each other. It was important that everyone get an opportunity to speak to every topic, but without us creating polite silences while we waited for the next person to take their turn. In other words, the intention was to create a relaxed but vibrant discussion between women that would provide a point of identification for female viewers at home.

After the taping it was a waiting game. The edited 'pilot' program had to do the rounds of the network, being shown to program directors in every state, as well as to the upper echelon at PBL, the magazine arm of company. I was concerned it might fall flat because, from my limited experience in television, it lacked production quality. There had been little pre-production or 'styling', and to me it felt raw and a bit rough around the edges.

Nevertheless, a month later, we got the call that the show was 'on' and would start production early the following year, going to air at the beginning of the ratings period. I was astounded, but also excited at the prospect. To celebrate we were to be invited to a boardroom lunch on the third floor of the Nine Network's main building in Artarmon. That meant we had really made the big time – I chuckled mightily to myself. David and I had met for the first time in this very building, more than thirty years earlier. He was working as the associate producer of a family situation comedy series called *The Godfathers* and I had joined the publicity department after completing my training at the *Weekly*. My ultimate ambition was to join the Channel 9 newsroom as a reporter. Three months after I arrived, David asked me out, right there in the studio where we had just taped the talk show pilot. Just thinking of the path our lives had taken in the decades since that moment, it was not lost on me that I had come full circle.

Next came the contract negotiations. Having worked for the ABC for nine years I had a pretty fair idea of what an average television presenter is paid, but this was different. Our show was to be one hour, live to air, five days a week, and presumably it would not be expensive to produce with its studio set and chat format. I knew that we could not demand a rate of pay like Kerri-Anne Kennerley's because her show is heavily sponsored and she is the sole host. Nevertheless, I was determined not to undersell myself. I knew that the network would negotiate hard and that they would keep the four of us apart during these negotiations. David came with me to meet Channel 9's director of daytime television, and we were both surprised at just how little they were prepared to pay. We managed to push the fee up a tad; the network also agreed to pay for my accommodation and weekly airfares from Bathurst, where we have a farm, to Sydney. So we shook hands on the deal. A contract was to be posted out the following week.

I kept in regular communication with my co-hosts, but we steered clear of discussing the delicate topic of our individual contracts. I secretly wondered, though, if they were being paid as little as me. I rationalised that if the show took off I could renegotiate a much better deal for the following year.

The boardroom lunch date was set, and the atmosphere was one of high spirits and excitement. French champagne was opened and we were introduced to half a dozen top-level executives who would be involved on the periphery of the production. I can't remember the menu, but

I do recall that almost all of us – Indira being the definite exception – drank far too much wine, and were very loud and totally over the top. The heady combination of the situation we found ourselves in and our underlying nervous energy put us in a skittish mood. I wondered, with hindsight, if our behaviour at this lunch had any bearing on what ultimately happened. I do recall that when dessert was offered I feigned horror and asked the waiter if there was to be a cheese course. The nerve of me, flaunting my French influences. He scurried back to the kitchen and produced a platter of cheeses for us to share – everyone seemed to think it was hilarious, but of course it was very bad manners. I cringe when I think of it now.

No contracts arrived. Week after week there were emails of apology and explanation and the starting date for pre-production was moved further back. First to March, then April and then May. It was a nightmare for all of us because our careers and lives were 'on hold' during the drawn-out process. Channel 9 had 'leaked' a press release giving details about the program and the names of the four panel members; this was picked up at the ABC, and Shelley Horton was given her marching orders. Cleo and Indira had both knocked back other job offers, while I had cancelled various walking tours that I had planned to lead that year. When the network moved the launch date back to May I asked if it would be OK if I went ahead with a trek to Nepal that had been planned for more than a year. Management readily agreed, as long as I was back in Sydney by early May. It meant changing the dates of the tour, and we lost half our starters. I was cranky but resigned to the fact that I had to fit in with Channel 9's demands if I wanted to retain my position on the show.

The day before I flew out there was yet another apologetic email with grave assurances that there would be a contract waiting for me to sign when I returned in two weeks. I was confident it would be all right in the end, and pleased to have a distraction in the meantime. I thought the trip would energise me and put me in great mental and physical shape for the daunting task ahead. I dreamed the show would be a runaway success, and fantasised in a bemused way about becoming a daytime TV star. Australia's answer to Oprah or Barbara Walters. Fame and fortune were just around the corner.

3

The treks I lead in the Himalayas are botanical in focus, bringing Australians to regions where the flora is quite extraordinary. These mountains contain the greatest diversity of plants in the world. I have taken groups to lush valleys in northern India and also into Nepal to see wild musk roses, alpine meadows of primula and ranunculus, and forests of rhododendrons laden with great clusters of bloom. We walk through villages as we climb for sometimes seven or eight hours a day, to remote campsites where we enjoy the snow-covered peaks and the rushing rivers which punctuate the landscape. Trekking lifts me out of my comfort zone and challenges me, both mentally and physically. At times the climbing at altitude can be quite tough, and as a group we bond because we support each other in the struggle to reach camp every evening.

The political situation in Nepal had been very unsettled for several months before we arrived, and Maoist guerrillas were reportedly all through the areas where we would be walking. Even in the capital there was a lot of unrest, with two small bombs going off in the shopping area several hundred metres from our hotel. As a result of the last-minute cancellations, it was a small group of six that headed out from

Kathmandu towards the Annapurna mountains. We set off in glorious sunshine, tramping along goat tracks and chattering enthusiastically about the scenery and the people we met along the way.

One of the aspects I most enjoy about these treks is the total escape from the modern world. While Kathmandu is a very civilised city with modern hotels and all the facilities – international television access, the internet and mobile phones – once you reach a certain altitude, all the conveniences of modern life disappear. It's bliss. I am accustomed to reading the newspaper every day – and love a chance to read a foreign newspaper like the *Himalayan Times* and *Kantipur National Daily* – yet I also relish escaping from the news of the world altogether. It's liberating not to hear a single radio broadcast or watch the nightly TV news for ten days straight. And being without email and phone access is just as exhilarating. Sometimes, in the back of my mind, I worry that some major world event – a war, an act of terrorism or a natural disaster – may be unfolding while we climb the mountains, totally oblivious. I also have moments when I worry about my family's inability to contact me should there be a crisis, but again I rationalise this anxiety, knowing that there are enough caring adult family members to support each other should anything go wrong. I have passed the stage of feeling indispensable.

This trip went off without a hitch, and we arrived back at the hotel in Kathmandu eight days later, high from our adventure. No matter how many times I've led such expeditions, I always get a happy rush of endorphins when the walk is over. It's a combination of exercise, healthy food, fresh air and a huge sense of accomplishment. After celebrating with the rest of the group over a bottle of the local beer, I showered for the first time since we had set out for the mountains, scrubbing my scalp and soaking my aching feet in the tub. Dressed in clean clothes, I sauntered down to the lobby and logged on to the internet at one of the complimentary guest computers.

There were dozens of emails in my inbox, but the first one I clicked on was from our hard-working Channel 9 producer.

I spoke to David this morning and he suggested that you might get this email before you arrive home and whilst it would have been better to do this over the phone I wanted to fill you in on what's happening with the chat show before you read it in a newspaper.

Unfortunately the show has been put on hold indefinitely so will not be going ahead in May as promised.

We are all terribly disappointed about it, but of course we also know the nature of this industry. I wanted to express how sorry I am that it has happened after such a long road and also wanted to say a huge thank you for being so patient and understanding. You especially have been very helpful in moving dates for your tours and trips to France and I thank you very much for that.

I am sorry to be the bearer of bad news whilst you are still overseas but I hope to catch you on the phone if possible to talk further. I would also like to take the girls out to lunch for one last 'hurrah' next Tuesday, so if you are in Sydney let me know.

Although I was upset that I had been kept dangling so long – not to mention the fact that I had reorganised my entire year's schedule to fit in with Channel 9's demands – I wasn't as devastated as I might have been under the circumstances. When I spoke to David, he was anticipating that I would be shattered. I wasn't. When the producer said it was 'the nature of the business' I knew exactly what she meant, and I didn't take the cancellation personally, as a rejection of me, or as a sense of failure. In fact, I laughed to myself and went to the bar for a beer with my friends.

When I returned to Australia in early May, I communicated briefly with one of the executives in change of the situation, asking for some form of financial compensation for the inconvenience and lost work opportunities of the past six months. I knew the others were doing the same. He responded by saying that the show hadn't been axed, that it was 'on hold' and that he hoped it would be reactivated later that year. I knew this was a load of nonsense; if a show has been dropped before it even begins then from my perspective it's dead in the water. So much for my fantasies about being a daytime TV star!

After the debacle of the cancelled chat show, I put to rest any thoughts of doing more television.

4

My forays into the world of TV, documentary-making and radio have always been a sideline to my primary career as a journalist and writer. Although I have relished the opportunity to spread my wings and explore these other possibilities, writing has won out in the end.

Most of my work has been straightforward journalism, from my days as a young reporter to my twenty-five years as a health and gardening writer. However in the past few years I've mainly written stories from my own life. The path of self-revelation is not one I chose deliberately, or with any consideration of its inherent risks. I stumbled onto it naïvely when I first recounted my adventures as a lone woman in France for a travel memoir, *Au Revoir*. As my story developed and became more complex and difficult, so did the writing of the subsequent books, and the impact on my marriage was profound.

I am certain there are very few husbands who would tolerate a wife writing honest accounts of her infidelities for anyone to read. Some days when I stop to think about it, I myself can barely believe that's what I've done. I'm not only amazed by my own conduct, I'm amazed that David has weathered the storms of these last few years and that somehow our marriage has survived. It's difficult enough living through the experience of a huge marital upheaval without having to re-live it in print, then re-live it again through the media.

The burning question for many readers and interviewers is why. Why expose your dirty linen and share your pain with the rest of the world by documenting it all for publication? Why not, is my usual response. After all, it's love, life and the whole damn thing. What happened to me and David is just part of the human condition, and many couples have been through similar rough times in their relationships.

Sweeping the fact of my affairs under the carpet felt to me like denial. I needed to write the whole story down, to get it out there in the open. Documenting the many things that happened to me after I turned fifty was a form of therapy, especially when I tried to explain my feelings to myself, and to reflect on how they affected my other relationships. The writing process helped me to reach some sort of understanding of why this period of tumult had ever happened.

At first, David was opposed to the idea of my writing about our life together, and while I was working on my second memoir, *Last Tango in Toulouse*, he fought against it. However, by the time I came to write *The Long Hot Summer* he was totally onside. He believed it was a story worth telling, and he supported me through the writing and the subsequent harrowing publicity. The tricky part has always been living life while writing about it almost at the same time. It's like walking a tightrope, balancing the feelings of close family members while being as candid as possible at the same time.

By the time *The Long Hot Summer* was published in mid-2005, David and I were both exhausted by the entire process. We had decided not to separate, but we had good patches and bad patches, days and weeks when we got along extremely well, followed by periods when I privately believed that our reconciliation was a mistake, a waste of time. I don't know why I imagined that our new life together would simply go along without a hitch. I should have realised that the healing process and the readjustment would take a long, long time and that there would always be moments when bad memories would come flooding back. Some things simply could never be forgiven and some aspects of our relationship would never be the same again.

David's trust in me had been badly shaken. He knew that I wanted to keep going back to France, and he simply didn't feel confident that I wouldn't slip back in to my old love affairs or even initiate new ones once I was out of sight and such a long way from home (and his watchful eye). Nothing I could say or do reassured him; with a sinking heart, I gradually realised that his trust in me might never be fully restored. Some people would say that a marriage without trust can't survive, but we have managed to deal with it by being very open. David lets me know how he's feeling. I listen. We talk some more. Keeping the lines of communication open is our greatest priority.

When I think about it I am aware that more women than men have been in the same position as David, dealing with a partner who has strayed. Most men would be inclined to end a marriage if they discovered a straying wife, but women are generally more conciliatory and prepared to forgive their husbands and move forward. David has been remarkable in his ability to deal with it all, although at times – even now – he will suddenly get angry or upset remembering something that happened during those dark few years, and the pain will bubble up to the surface again. I find this very difficult and confronting but I know only too well that it's a healthy release for him. A normal reaction.

The curious thing is that he doesn't get angry with me about the events of the past. He's inclined to blame other people and sometimes even himself for the situation that developed. While he doesn't imagine I was an innocent bystander, he certainly believes I was caught up in the heat of the moment and was not deliberately setting out to destroy our marriage.

We both work on the theory that negotiation and renegotiation are what it's all about. We can't just stagnate and expect our marriage to survive. We must recognise and acknowledge each other's changing needs and desires and try to meet them as much as possible. It's been a wake-up call and we have responded, I hope, by becoming more aware of each other. More tuned in to each other. In many ways, our relationship is now much better than it ever has been. It has evolved through pain and difficulty.

Our children have been very loyal and supportive to us both, given that it must have been stressful for them when it looked as though their parents might go their separate ways. Now it's a subject never discussed at family gatherings, and I don't believe that's because it's become 'taboo' – it's just that they're thoroughly bored by the whole business. They have their own busy, demanding lives and any problems that we are having are now for us to solve alone. As a family we have also moved along.

On a day-to-day basis nothing much has changed. Our roles have remained the same although, to his credit, David has taken on a lot of the domestic aspects of living at the farm, probably because I have been away so much over the last few years. It's quite a convivial life we lead here at Yetholme. He brings me tea in bed every morning – proper leaf tea, brewed in a pot, never a teabag. Strained and stirred in a china cup and accompanied by a thin slice of homemade bread and butter.

Getting him onto the tractor can sometimes be a bit of a struggle. He's totally unmechanically minded, and refuses to even try to learn the basics of tractor maintenance, so it's up to me to get the large machine out of the shed, check the diesel, oil, water, hydraulics and air filter, and make sure the height and speed settings are appropriate. I do a quick run around checking for obstacles – fallen branches or large dog bones – and pack away any hoses that might get tangled in the mower's blades. When it's all set to go, David strides out in his protective gear and proceeds with the task at hand. He is meticulous and does a wonderful job but it's all a bit of a gala performance. When he's finished, I clean the tractor down, blowing the loose grass away with a compressor, then park it back in the shed until next time.

But to be completely fair to him, David has embraced a lot of the chores I used to do when the children were growing up. Shopping is just one example. He seems to love cruising the supermarket aisles looking for bargains, comparing weights and prices and brands. I have always shopped on the run, without a list and throwing items into the trolley at whim. He loves being in charge of an orderly, planned shopping trip, and carefully unpacks everything when he gets it home. The pantry is always well-stocked.

I divide my day between gardening, cooking and writing. David does all his emails and work phone calls in the morning and then spends the afternoon in Bathurst doing the shopping and going to the gym. He has type 2 diabetes and needs to exercise frequently to keep his condition under control. When he returns home from town he tends to wander back to his office and his computer, and he gets so caught up that I sometimes feel he's forgotten I'm there at all. I send an email from my computer to his: *Do you remember me? I'm that red-headed woman on the other side of the house and I feel like a gin and tonic.* He emerges, smiling, and we share a drink before dinner and the evening news.

I try my best to introduce a little fun into our quiet life. I insist that we have a meal out from time to time, although it's a struggle because he claims to prefer home-cooked meals to those served in restaurants. Luckily, we both love the local Chinese restaurant and there are also a few interesting cafes in town where we can take a bottle of wine. I keep my eye out for good movies coming to our local cinema, and for the plays and concerts that often tour up from Sydney to Bathurst's excellent entertainment centre. I have to push for these outings because, like a lot of men in his age group, David has become more of a homebody in his later years. He'd rather sit near the fire watching his favourite television series than make the effort to go out. I tend to force him.

I expect our life together and our relationship is not that different from those of other couples who have been together for more than thirty-five years. We are both still working and active, and we travel a lot – usually going our own separate ways – but our lifestyle at home is very settled, and to others it may even appear rather boring at times. In essence, we are trying to get on with enjoying life, even though we have had our difficulties and sadnesses. The same as most people.

5

 'I want to grow old without facelifts . . . I want to have the courage to be loyal to the face I've made.'

—Marilyn Monroe

These words – so bravely spoken, but so sad to read now – sum up how most younger women feel about cosmetic surgery. When your face is still smooth and line-free, you have absolutely no idea how you will feel when the first major signs of ageing appear. Poor Marilyn never had the chance to live to a ripe old age, and we will never know how she would have looked at sixty or seventy had she stuck to her guns and resisted plastic surgery.

When I was younger I felt exactly the same way as she did. I was critical of women who felt so insecure about themselves that they would submit to the surgeon's knife in order to cling to their fading youth and beauty. I had read Germaine Greer and was a big fan of her take on how women had been manipulated by the male-dominated medical profession and the pharmaceutical and cosmetic industries. My views were political as well as emotional. I didn't like the idea of being swept up in a tide of vain women incapable of accepting the natural results of living their lives, who allowed themselves to be 'got at' by the media and the advertising industry. I continued to feel this way very strongly – until I hit fifty! It's easy to be judgemental about all sorts of things until you find yourself affected by them.

Genetics has a lot to do with how our faces age. Those of us with Celtic complexions who grew up as beach babes in the fifties and sixties have paid the price in later life. At menopause, our skin also starts to deteriorate rapidly as our hormonal levels drop. The combination of the two effects can be truly disturbing.

For me, this sudden facial ageing really started in my early fifties, and accelerated at such a rate that I became alarmed. Until then my face had been comparatively unlined and my jawline smooth, but it seemed as though overnight I developed pouchy jowls, and my face began to look worn and weather-beaten. No amount of cosmetic creams or make-up could cover what I feared was rapidly advancing old age.

Out of curiosity, I experimented with a Botox treatment, enduring a series of injections to smooth the lines on my forehead between my eyebrows. Although it wasn't painful, it was expensive, and I didn't like the sensation of numbness that accompanied the effect. I decided I would rather have a few frown lines than an expressionless forehead.

But my anxiety about my face falling apart returned with full force when the daytime television show was proposed, and I saw some of the pilot footage. While I was more than prepared to acknowledge I was at least fifteen years older than any of the other women in the auditions, I felt miserable that in the close-ups I often looked saggy and tired – not so much when I was talking and animated, but when I was in repose.

Like so many women of my age I stood in front of the mirror in the bathroom, and pulled back the skin on either side of my face to try to imagine how it would look if I had a facelift. I liked the 'tightened up' me and started to make tentative enquiries about plastic surgeons and the various procedures that were available.

David disagreed entirely with my perception of what was happening to my face, but then again he rarely notices if I put an auburn rinse in my hair or buy a new dress. He was quite horrified when I first suggested I might do something 'surgical' to pull my face back into line. But in November 2004 after some research, I decided on a cosmetic surgeon and booked an appointment anyway. I wasn't prepared for the clandestine nature of the industry. Apparently people having 'work done' insist upon total discretion and often husbands and boyfriends are kept in the dark completely. When the receptionist phoned the day before to confirm my appointment – I wasn't at home at the time – she refused to say who she was or why she was calling to David, who became irritated by all the secrecy. When I arrived at the doctor's rooms I was ushered into a private waiting room just in case someone who knew me arrived at the same time. I found this cloak and dagger approach quite hilarious.

The surgeon took some 'before' photos and we discussed the various options. I didn't want a full facelift – I dislike that artificial, stretched look that I have seen on other women. I was a fifty-five-year-old grandmother and I was happy to look my age. I just wanted my ragged edges tidied up – the good old euphemism 'nip and tuck' was all that I desired. He recommended an 'S-Lift', which concentrates on the lower half of the face, mainly the jawline. It was proper surgery, requiring an overnight stay in hospital and an anaesthetic. It amazed me how quickly the whole thing was organised – almost before I had time for a moment's reflection I was getting ready to trot off to hospital.

I was told to buy some concentrated spray-on arnica, to squirt under my tongue several times a day in the weeks leading up to the surgery. Arnica is a fantastic natural antidote to bruising and my doctor believed that having a good dose of it in your system before the operation would help prevent any massive swelling as a reaction afterwards. I dutifully squirted the arnica in my mouth and cut back on my drinking, again to prevent a post-operative reaction.

As I lay in pre-op a few weeks later, I reminded the surgeon that I didn't want radical surgery, just a subtle effect – the bare minimum. He was drawing lines on my skin to follow with a scalpel. David had opposed my decision. A hospital phobic, he had nightmares about me having an anaesthetic and the possible complications that could arise. And what if I ended up looking like a gargoyle? Despite my growing reservations, it was far too late to change my mind.

When I woke, I felt fine, although I was told that I had suffered a minor reaction to the anaesthetic during the operation. I had a strap around my face but didn't feel any pain or even much discomfort. It seemed like a doddle. Although I was still a bit groggy, I got chatting to the woman in the next bed. She was recovering from a lumpectomy for breast cancer, and was visibly distressed and quite fearful about her outcome. She didn't ask the reason for my surgery, and I didn't volunteer it. By now I was on a fully fledged guilt trip. Here I was feeling comparatively bright and breezy after what had been an elective procedure based on vanity. There she was struggling to come to terms with the possibility that her operation may not have succeeded in ridding her body of cancer cells. She was facing both chemo and radiotherapy. I was going home to rest for a couple of days until the swelling went down, then to go merrily on with my life. It felt very wrong.

I was also keenly aware of the shortage of hospital beds for much more valid elective procedures. Lack of theatre time and post-operative beds is a major cause of our medical system's long waiting lists, and I couldn't help but wonder just how many plastic surgery procedures were clogging up the system. My surgery day had been booked within weeks of my initial consultation. It was a private hospital, but the theatre and my bed could have been put to better use. I wondered how the nursing staff felt about this situation, and that made me squirm even more. I was very keen to get home.

True to his word, the surgeon had gone gently with the knife and two weeks after the surgery it was virtually impossible to detect that anything very much had been done. I noticed a much smoother jawline – those little pouchy bits on my chin, directly below my mouth, had vanished, but otherwise I looked very much the same, perhaps just a little less haggard. I told quite a few friends but then stopped mentioning it, and nobody commented. Nobody said 'Gosh, you look fantastic', or 'Have you been on a holiday? You look so relaxed', or 'How do you keep yourself looking so young?'. I certainly didn't look thirty-five, or even forty-five. I still looked like a woman in her fifties, and for that I was grateful.

What I didn't realise then is that if you seriously want to intervene in the ageing process, it's like being on a treadmill – very hard to get off. During my six-week post-op visit, the receptionists and assistants in the surgeon's glamorous rooms were effusive about the results – that's their job. They immediately suggested that I should get some Botox and Restylane fillers to 'go with' the S-Lift. They talked about me coming back regularly for more treatments – suggesting the area under my eyes could do with some work and that I could also have work done on my neck and chest area. There's the rub. If you have a facelift you have to be prepared for the fact that it won't match the age of the rest of your body – your neck and your décolletage and your arms and your hands. Since my nip and tuck all those other parts of me have started to crumble, and quite frankly I no longer care. Well, I *do* care because I wish my skin was young and smooth and firm again. But I am finally reconciled to the inevitability of my physical decline.

6

The happiest time of my life was when my children were growing up. I loved every aspect of motherhood and from the age of twenty-two defined myself by that role. Looking back, I probably wasn't the best mother in the world, but at the time I certainly felt very much in control. I loved being the mistress of my home, organising the kids, cooking the meals and beavering away in my garden. I always worked in paid employment as well, but that too was a pleasurable experience. I was young and energetic and full of the joy of life.

It surprised me when our four children, as teenagers, opted for serious relationships rather than flitting from boyfriend to girlfriend. They all had a couple of minor flings during the experimental stages that young people go through when they first discover the opposite sex, but within a few years appeared to settle into relationships with one 'special' person. They wanted commitment and permanency. Some parents might have discouraged this trend. I could have pushed them to concentrate on their careers and play the field rather than sliding so comfortably into domesticity, but I didn't.

Nevertheless, living in the Blue Mountains meant that once they finished high school they needed to leave home to pursue further educational and career opportunities. Tony went to an apprenticeship in Sydney, Miriam moved to Canberra to study at university, Aaron travelled north to Lismore to study horticulture, and eventually our youngest son, Ethan, did the same.

Tony was the last to fall in love, the first to marry. He and his beautiful girlfriend Simone had a fairytale wedding in the garden. They lived and worked in Sydney, both had successful and well-paid careers and were planning to save for their first home. The future was rosy.

Miriam had a steady boyfriend when she left home to go to university to study arts/law and then communications, but after that relationship broke up she fell in love with Rick, and in the last year of her degree she gave birth to Eamonn, my first grandchild. I was delighted, but also somewhat surprised when they announced the pregnancy. To both David and me, Miriam always appeared such a focused career girl, an academic overachiever who would probably end up in some high-powered city job, delaying partnership and parenthood until her late thirties. Not so. Miriam and Rick moved back to the Mountains – then to Bathurst – and over the next decade had three more beautiful boys, Samuel, Theo and Augustus. Eventually they moved to Adelaide, so that Miriam could follow her passion for natural childbirth by enrolling in the three-year Bachelor of Midwifery degree offered by Flinders University. She's a fine example of how her generation embraces change without fear: from law to communications to midwifery – I sometimes wonder what she will do next!

Aaron left school before the HSC and worked as a trainee landscaper – inspired, I suspect, by my passion for gardens and plants. At the time he had a steady girlfriend and several of his friends had decided to do university degrees in Lismore, so he enrolled in a TAFE horticulture course to formalise his qualifications. For various reasons Aaron's friends gradually dropped out of their studies and returned to the Mountains. He was lonely and, I now realise, quite depressed but he stuck it out. When he returned home he reconnected with Lorna, a girl from his high school days. They set up house together and Aaron continued to work and study. Like Aaron, Lorna was a very hard worker, grounded and responsible, and a lot less wild than his previous girlfriends. Once again I was surprised when they announced that Lorna was pregnant. She looked a little shocked too – it was unplanned – but Aaron was over the moon. Hamish was born not long after Miriam's second child, Sam, so suddenly we had three lovely little boys in the family. Two years later – it was the year I spent six months living alone in France – Aaron and Lorna produced their second child, our first granddaughter, Ella Mary.

Ethan, our youngest by five years, grew up even more quickly than his older siblings. He left school early and studied music in Sydney for a year, then became involved in a relationship with Lynne, who was keen to study horticulture and the environment. They moved in together, somehow surviving on a very modest income, and formed a tight-knit team from the beginning. They travelled north to study and lived frugally, even managing to save for an ancient car on their student allowances. After graduating, they moved back to the Mountains and – wanting to inspire them and to broaden their horizons – I suggested that they save up and go to stay in the little village house that David and I had bought in south-west France. Save they did. They moved back into our house, worked three or four jobs at a time, and within six months had cobbled together their airfares and spending money. I was delighted, believing this would open a door to the world for them. Even though I was thrilled with my grandchildren, part of me was a little sad that Miriam and Aaron would almost certainly be tied down for many years to come with the responsibilities of parenting when their friends of a similar age were forging ahead in their careers and travelling the world. So I really wanted Ethan and Lynne to travel and to enjoy their youth to the full.

They headed off to France and I went off to lead one of my trekking tours. I was staying in a small hotel high in the Indian Himalayas when a call came through from Miriam with the news that Ethan and Lynne were expecting a child. To say I was stunned would be an understatement. When I managed to get through to them they told me Lynne had been feeling unwell since they first arrived in France, and that eventually she had tests which revealed her pregancy. They were both quite happy, though naturally a little surprised by the prospect, and unfortunately it meant that they would have to come home several months early because the airlines won't allow anyone over thirty-two weeks pregnant to travel on an international flight.

Lynne often felt unwell during her pregnancy but, despite that, she and Ethan had a fantastic time in Frayssinet, where they were embraced by the local community. Then they flew home – Lynne barely looked pregnant at all – and seven weeks later tiny Isabella was born. She was the smallest baby I had ever seen – terrifyingly small – with a thatch of red hair and translucent skin. She was exquisite, but something about her seemed not quite right. In France they had been warned that various prenatal test results indicated that their unborn child was at risk of a 'chromosomal disorder', but the paediatrician in the delivery room declared that she was 'small but perfectly formed and normal'. The whole family adored her from the first moment. It turned out that Isabella did indeed have problems, which only emerged gradually, becoming more serious with time. However Ethan and Lynne bravely went on to have second child – this time a large and healthy boy. They named him Caius, the first name of Julius Caesar, quite a moniker for our youngest grandchild to grow into.

In 2005, a few months after *The Long Hot Summer* was published, Ethan and his family came to live with us at the farm while they were saving for a house of their own. The plan was that they would build on the five-acre block at the back of the farm, which is separated from the main part of the property by the old Sydney road. We loved the idea that they would be living nearby. It meant that we could help with the children, while Ethan and Lynne could help keep an eye on the farm when we were away travelling for work.

The local council had other ideas. Our farm had once been in the Evans Shire which, like so many regional councils across the state, was amalgamated with a larger council nearby (Bathurst City) to form a super council. The rationale was that that the administrative costs would be greatly reduced. After the amalgamation there was a moratorium on subdivisions in our region and, in principle, I agree it was necessary. It's disheartening to see productive farmland being carved up into lifestyle building blocks. However, our vacant block was certainly not productive, being covered with scrub, weeds and noxious pine tree seedlings from surrounding state forests. It needed a lot of environmental management, and Ethan and Lynne would have been just the couple to restore it brilliantly, with their horticultural and environmental bush management qualifications. When it became clear that the council was not about to make any exceptions, they continued to save with a view to buying a house back in the Blue Mountains when they could afford it, and in the meantime they lived with us.

By this time, Isabella had been diagnosed with a range of quite severe disabilities, and was in need of constant care and attention, day and night. David and I had become accustomed to living alone as a couple, and we knew we would have to adjust to having a young family in the house, especially given Isabella's problems and the recent strains on our marriage. David was worried that it might be stressful to have so many people suddenly living under the same roof, but I thought it would be good for us all. I have always enjoyed the atmosphere of a lively house full of people, and having children around is very grounding.

Child locks were fitted to the kitchen cupboards and the pantry shelves were rearranged so that only unbreakable items were on the lower shelves. Like many men after they reach middle age, David isn't relaxed about change. I was aware of him muttering and mumbling because he 'couldn't find anything' in the pantry, and struggling to unlatch the childproof locks on the cupboards. In recent years he had taken over the laundry, doing my washing as well as his own. Suddenly the laundry was filled with buckets and basins for soaking – both Isabella and Caius were in nappies and Isabella's feeding pump sometimes popped apart, leaking the pungent formula onto sheets and towels – and there was a mountain of washing to be done every day. The family room was filled with children's toys and various large pieces of equipment used for Isabella's daily occupational therapy and physiotherapy. Everything was very neatly stowed away and not scattered underfoot, but having a two-year-old bouncing around in his pyjamas during David's precious television news time was a bit unsettling for him at first.

But I just loved it. Even though I was working in my office most of the day, I could come out and spend some time with Isabella or Caius to free up their mother if she needed to do something else. Lynne is a super-organised, efficient young woman; she couldn't have survived the difficulties of caring for a disabled child and a toddler at the same time without being on top of everything. We took turns in planning menus and cooking. Lynne is very strict about Caius's diet – much as I was with my children when they were kids.

As well as travelling back to the Blue Mountains for his job, Ethan did a tremendous amount of work around the farm. Like all the farms around us we have been suffering from the drought – years of it – and our water supply from the spring had become fragile. Ethan encouraged us to abandon the idea of keeping stock while water reserves were so low, and he redesigned and rebuilt the fencing so that when the day finally comes that we are once again able to put animals out to graze, they won't be able to walk through the wetland or trample and despoil the creek or the dams that flow into it. He also eradicated the broom and blackberry that had started to proliferate in various paddocks and set aside an area for natural bush regeneration. The trees that have seeded on that hillside are now well over three metres tall.

Living in an extended family requires tolerance and compromise. For twenty-six years while the children were growing up, my mother, Muriel, lived with us at Leura, and it required a lot of give and take from all of us to make it work. Having our young family at the farm reminded me of how carefully the situation had to be managed. It was harmonious most of the time, but there were some hair-trigger moments. Ethan needed to get up extremely early to shower for work. David was also in the habit of rising early, to make his ritual three cups of coffee that allow him to 'ease into' the day. Our water pressure at the farm is pretty dodgy, reliant on a pump to send water into the kitchen and bathroom. Some mornings David inadvertently had the taps flowing in the kitchen during Ethan's shower, leaving the poor boy shivering under a pathetic cold drizzle. Words were spoken. Yet this living arrangement, so common in previous generations when young married couples often stayed with their parents until they found their feet financially, ultimately became very agreeable and cosy.

David loves small children, but doesn't have a natural aptitude with them. This interlude enabled him to develop a delightful relationship with his youngest grandson. One of David's chores is to care for our flocks of geese, ducks and chicken, which involves releasing the geese to graze every morning, feeding and watering the remaining birds and collecting the eggs. In the evening the eggs are collected, water freshened, and geese rounded up for the night. Caius took to helping his grandfather with this task, and the sight of the two of them striding purposefully down to the poultry yard together every morning, each holding a walking stick, did my heart good.

Having Isabella in the house somehow seemed to mellow David. It's impossible to ignore her presence in any room – not that she's particularly demanding. It's just that she needs a lot of interaction and affection, and I realised that David was paying more attention to her than I had ever seen him give our own children. Not in a practical sense, but in terms of making eye contact with her, talking to her and keeping her company in the back room while the rest of us were busy with other things. We became very, very attached to both the children and accustomed to the house being full of life and noise and action.

We would have been happy, I'm sure, to continue living this way indefinitely, but after nearly two years, Isabella's deteriorating health forced her family to move back to Blackheath, where they were closer to the hospital where she receives treatment.

7

Beautiful Isabella, with her alabaster skin and long red hair, is a joy and a great worry to her parents. Isabella's journey has been a rocky one, probably from the moment of conception. There is no obvious explanation for why she failed to thrive in utero, no illness, no accident, no set of circumstances that would cause placenta and baby to remain so tiny. In her young life she seems to have spent almost as much time in hospital as she has at home, hooked up to a feeding pump that delivers vitamin-enriched formula directly into her stomach via a valve in the side of her small, thin body. The fact that she survived is, I suppose, a miracle in itself, due to the advances of modern medicine – which make life possible for infants who in previous generations would certainly have died – and to the devotion of her parents.

Having Isabella in our family has quite radically changed the way I feel about fundamental life and death issues. If you had asked me a decade ago what I thought about a child who couldn't walk, talk or sit upright for more than a couple of moments, who couldn't chew or swallow food, and who had hearing and vision problems and therefore wasn't capable of functioning in any way like a normal, healthy child,

I would have said that particular child would be better off dead. I certainly don't feel that way now.

Isabella's parents are fiercely independent and have coped with the care of their disabled child without asking for or expecting much help, even from their immediate families. From the moment it became obvious, around the age of about six months, that Isabella's problems were much more complex than just a failure to thrive, they have assumed the mantle of responsibility and done so in an amazingly positive, good-natured and accepting manner. They have never complained about their lot even though since her birth seven years ago they have not enjoyed a peaceful night's sleep, and have the constant worry of a child whose future appears very uncertain. I have enormous admiration for them both.

Medically, Isabella's condition falls into the category of 'global developmental delays'. This is just another way of saying she has a whole cluster of different problems, some connected and some that stand alone. It took more than a year before the various government departments that support families with disabled children would offer any assistance because there had been no definitive diagnosis. In spite of testing for a wide range of disorders and syndromes, there simply wasn't a convenient label they could put on Isabella, and therefore she fell through the cracks in terms of qualifying for support.

Eventually it was acknowledged that she wasn't simply suffering from delayed development and that there were many more serious symptoms that would require ongoing treatment for the rest of her life. She needed the care of so many different specialists – starting with paediatricians and gastroenterologists, and including dieticians, neurologists, speech pathologists, physiotherapists and occupational therapists. The list goes on.

Isabella cannot ingest food normally, so finding the best sustenance for her has been a nightmare. She is fed through a tube, and her digestive system can't tolerate rich formulas, so there is a constant process of finetuning going on in the hope that she will continue growing despite the fact that the liquid pumped into her tummy is better suited to nourishing a newborn than a seven-year-old. She has grown, certainly, but she is much, much smaller than she should be for her age. Her legs, in particular, are very short and finding clothes that fit her is always a problem.

During the period leading up to the age of four Isabella made steady, if extremely slow, progress. She could sit for more than an hour at a time, was interested in everything around her, and had started rolling around and getting up onto all fours. We all felt certain that she was on the verge of learning to crawl. She was having intensive physiotherapy, including spending increasingly lengthy periods in a standing frame that had been designed and built specifically for her size and her needs. There is a lovely aspect to all this and it's about volunteering. Groups of retired men – men who often have been carpenters or builders during their careers – give their time to build customised equipment for disabled children. They create special seats with trays so that the children can be well supported while playing with toys that are designed to stimulate their senses. They adapt beds and cots and wheelchairs to make them more suitable for the needs of a particular child. They construct standing frames which force the child to carry their own weight on their legs and feet while preventing them from toppling over.

Isabella spent hours in her special standing frame and, while we questioned that she would ever walk, we knew that this daily exercise was strengthening her legs and helping them to grow. Then something devastating happened. Isabella started to have seizures. At first they were like little flutterings of the eye, but gradually they increased in intensity and frequency, and she was diagnosed with epilepsy. This was the beginning of a downward spiral. As the seizures became worse Isabella started to lose her hard-fought-for milestones. The length of time she could sit unaided diminished, and she started falling over. Once she had been quite capable of lowering herself gently to the ground when she felt too tired to keep sitting up, but now she just flopped down. She required a protective helmet to prevent her from damaging her skull as she fell.

Isabella also suffers from a disorder called cyclic vomiting, which means that every few weeks her system rebels, and she simply can't hold her food down for three or four days, or even longer. This results in extended stays in hospital because she can easily become dehydrated and unable to absorb the medication which protects her against seizures, thus putting her at risk of having a major 'event'. Lynne stays all day and night with her during these hospital visits, in a small fold-down bed provided by the hospital. She gets up early in the morning and dashes back to their house in Blackheath to organise Caius while Ethan is getting ready for work. Caius goes to pre-school two days a week, but if he's having an at-home day he goes back to the children's ward with his mother and they keep Isabella company until his father has returned from work. Lynne drives him home, staying to have dinner because the hospital does not provide meals for parents, and then, no matter how tired she may be, she drives back to the hospital to spend the night with her daughter. Some nights Ethan sleeps at the hospital instead to give Lynne a break and some time alone with Caius. It's an exhausting juggling act.

Lynne keeps a daily diary in which she records everything that happens with Isabella. Her feeds, her medications, her bowel and bladder movements, her sleep and her general state of mind. Often little Isabella is happy and will appear engaged and interested, making eye contact and smiling broadly. At other times she is distressed by severe seizures or the nausea that is part of the cyclic vomiting. It's heartbreaking.

One aspect of this journey that has troubled me has been the attitudes of some – though certainly not all – members of the medical profession. Initially there seemed to be a lack of faith in Lynne and Ethan because they were young, inexperienced parents. During a couple of consultations when they reported their observations about Isabella, their version of events was doubted. Indeed there were suggestions that they had exaggerated the seriousness of Isabella's condition, or embellished her reactions to certain feeding regimes or medications. This was outrageous, given that as her parents they were living and breathing her problems night and day while the 'experts' were only seeing her for ten or fifteen minutes at a time. It was in response to this that Lynne decided to keep her detailed diary.

At one point, unconvinced that they were making accurate reports, one doctor wanted Isabella to be admitted to hospital for several weeks so she could be kept under observation. Lynne and Ethan took turns to stay with her and it didn't take long for the nurses, and then finally the doctor, to agree that Isabella's parents' description of her behaviour and reactions was totally accurate.

Lynne and Ethan decided to try for their second child when Isabella was about two and a half years old. They had been seeing a genetic counsellor to determine the odds of having another child with a disability, yet no definitive answer could be given. So they went ahead, feeling optimistic that this time their child would be healthy and normal. The geneticist was disapproving, feeling they were irresponsible for choosing to risk a pregnancy until given the all-clear. That could have taken years.

Lynne had a healthy pregnancy; the baby appeared one hundred percent fit in routine ultrasounds. Lynne and Ethan declined an amniocentesis at eighteen weeks because of the risk of miscarriage. This test is routinely used to check for genetic and congenital disorders, and was recommended by the geneticist. Again their decision was frowned upon. Confident in their own judgement they went ahead with a homebirth under the supervision of a midwife. Caius was born blissfully, without the slightest complication. It was such a joyful moment after what had been a tough few years.

During the course of Isabella's treatment her parents also declined surgical intervention. There is an operation that can prevent a child from vomiting; called fundoplication, it literally means that the upper curve of the stomach is wrapped around the esophagus and stitched. Ethan and Lynne talked to a lot of people about this procedure, sought second and third opinions and decided, ultimately, that it would make Isabella's life more miserable because of the long periods of unrelieved nausea that would result. There was criticism of this decision.

They certainly were never opposed to surgical procedures per se – indeed last year she underwent a quite risky removal of her tonsils and adenoids in the hope it would help her breathe more easily. It was a success. But a recent operation under a general anaesthetic to remove some baby teeth which had become embedded in her gums resulted in a serious bout of pneumonia because she inhaled fluid at some point during the procedure. So everything brings a risk and therefore the decision to 'intervene' is at times a very troubling one.

It's my belief that parents should be listened to with much greater respect by the medical profession. Their decisions about the care of their child should also be honoured. There can be prejudice against young parents and there is sometimes an arrogant view that 'doctor knows best.' The doctor isn't the one getting up to the disabled child three times a night, or cradling them when they become distressed with constipation (from the medication) or bouts of violent vomiting.

Fortunately the vast majority of the specialists and paediatricians and nurses have been fantastic and have recognised the devotion with which Ethan and Lynne care for their precious daughter. Indeed the head nursing sister at our local hospital, where they used to take Isabella when they lived at the farm, told me they were the most wonderful parents she had encountered in all her decades of paediatric nursing. All we could do was give them our unqualified support in the knowledge that all their actions were directed at making Isabella's life as happy and comfortable as possible. Watching them cope with her continuing problems was certainly a reality check for me, balanced as it was against the more superficial and trivial aspects of my life and career.

8

Perhaps the Channel 9 executive had spoken the truth when he told me the daytime chat show would eventually go ahead, for one day in 2006 an email popped up in my inbox from the network's casting director, Henrie Stride. I assumed Henrie was a bloke, but she turned out to be a warm and friendly young woman, who told me the network was developing a new show, and that she wanted me to come in for an interview with Mia Freedman, the network's creative services director. Was this *The Watercooler* reincarnated, or something completely different? I was intrigued, and agreed to a meeting the following week.

I knew a little about Mia Freedman, who was a high-profile, clever young journalist who had trained on magazines at Australian Consolidated Press – the same background as my own. I was curious about her role at Channel 9, having followed the reports of the continuing upheavals at the network in the pages of the press. My memory of working at the station all those decades ago was of a very male-oriented environment, and I was aware that more recently the network had scored with programs like *The Footy Show*, which gave good ratings, and tried to compensate for failures in other areas, such as news, current affairs and the morning show.

For the interview I dressed in a strappy sun frock and high heels, having picked up a few clues from my previous casting experience, and decided to indulge in a spray tan to colour up my pale, freckly skin. Henrie met me in the foyer and once more I found myself in the lift heading for the executive suites on the third floor. Mia greeted me enthusiastically. A beautiful, delicate young woman with an open face and ready smile, she immediately engaged me, saying: 'You are hot, Mary. Just look at you. Do you mind me asking how old you are?'

I was thrown off guard, not by Mia asking my age but by her use of the word 'hot', which I had never heard in this context before (I would hear it many, many times over the next six months). It's youth-speak. When she said I was 'hot' I momentarily wondered if I was having yet another menopausal hot flush, but no, it turned out that she meant that I looked young and groovy for a grandmother of eight. I was off to a good start.

After chatting broadly about the concept for the new show I confessed to Mia and Henrie that as I don't watch daytime television and have never subscribed to pay TV, I hadn't seen the American program *The View*. But I told them I had a good friend in Bathurst who watched the show religiously. 'I learn a lot and I laugh' was the way my friend described it. Mia loved this take on it; she repeated it several times, smiling widely.

The program we discussed that day was to be called *The Catch-Up*, and sounded similar in most respects to the one that hadn't made it to air two years before. Mia and Henrie told me they planned to interview a lot of potential cast members but were not doing auditions, which was a great relief to me. They aimed to make up their mind quite quickly and let me know. Was I available the following year, five days a week?

I said yes.

Within three weeks they had narrowed down the field. Mia wrote:

Our casting blueprint was always: interesting, complex, smart, funny, warm women who are prepared to laugh at the world and themselves, be honest about their experiences and express their opinions.

Of all the women we spoke to about this project (and there were dozens), Henrie and I have whittled it down to four we adore – and you're one of those four.

I was the only survivor from the previous attempt to get a daytime chat show off the ground, and again I was to be the oldest. The other women cast were Libbi Gorr, aka Elle McFeast, by far the most experienced of us on-camera (she would be the anchor); a charming young radio host by the name of Zoe Sheridan; and Lisa Oldfield, wife of the former One Nation politician David Oldfield.

The concept was to throw together a mix of women of different ages and perspectives. We were told we had been chosen for what we could 'bring to the table' in terms of our varied lives and experiences.

It would seem that my main qualification, apart from my previous experience on ABC-TV's gardening show, was the fact that I was both a mother and grandmother, and had 'lived' life, especially in the last few years; Libbi, of course, had a high-profile media career and had recently had her first child at the age of forty-one; Zoe was enthusiastic and bubbly and had worked in radio and television, but she was also a single mother with two young daughters; Lisa was a successful businesswoman who had survived abuse as a teenager, and later a period of drug addiction, a succession of miscarriages and, more recently, aggressive skin cancer. Lisa's right-wing politics were also fundamental in her selection for the panel. There was a strong view from the production team that we needed to have lively debate on the show – that it would be ratings death if we were 'in violent agreement' – a term used often during the pre-production period.

Our different physical appearances were another factor in the casting: a blonde (Zoe), a brunette (Libbi), a redhead (me) and a sultry ebony (Lisa). Libbi's weight loss and association with Jenny Craig was appealing to women viewers at home with similar issues, and she was confident and sexy on camera. Lisa and Zoe were both stunningly good looking. I was to represent older viewers, but from the more youthful perspective of a typical baby boomer. I wondered why there had been no attempt to include a multicultural aspect to the casting – I had suggested several fantastic Aboriginal women who I knew could hold their own in a lively debate. Libbi's Jewishness was the only bit of ethnic variation in an otherwise very vanilla panel.

The game plan we were presented with was simple. During the early weeks of the program we should establish our individual characters and personalities by gradually revealing snippets of personal information about our lives. Then, when we had the viewers charmed and 'on side', we should be more forthcoming about our views and engage in high-spirited conversations, taking totally opposing sides on the issues of the day. We could become heated and express our views passionately, but we must never, ever get personal or unpleasant with each other on camera. We were to portray the image of four good friends who were genuinely fond of each other but quite comfortable agreeing to disagree. Not particularly easy given that we hadn't even met!

Mia, Henrie and the executive producer, Tara Smithson, were busy organising a get-together that would be spread over several days so that we could relax and get to know each other. We had been asked to submit a short biography so we could discover a little bit more about each other before we were brought together for that first meeting. It would also provide the basis of a media release when Nine's CEO, Eddie McGuire, and other network executives gave us the green light to proceed.

I sent a fairly dry, factual summation of my career highlights and some brief personal details, as did both Libbi and Zoe. Lisa sent a long and involved first-person account of her life and her various triumphs over adversity that read something like a misery memoir. It detailed childhood abuse, overcoming adversity to build a brilliant career, and a passionate romance with her husband, David Oldfield, based around a shared love of military history, scuba diving and pistol shooting. It would soon make its way into the wider world of the media.

Mia sent us an excited email detailing a three-day 'love-in', which would begin with two days of getting to know each other and workshopping our chemistry and conversation skills. On the third day, we would be given full hair and make-up, and a 'screen test' would be shot that would immediately be sent around the network for final approval.

'The mantra I have in my head for this show? I learn something and I laugh . . . that's the key,' Mia wrote.

Our first meeting was in the boardroom. Déjà vu. I was a little late because of a prior commitment that I couldn't change, so by the time I arrived my co-hosts were having a casual lunch of salads and sandwiches. It was the first time I had met the executive producer, Tara, who was bright and bubbly, but of course the most important mission was meeting and getting a handle on the other 'girls'.

'Aren't we having wine?' I asked, typically.

I thought it would help to relax everyone, and it certainly did, although Libbi abstained as she was still breastfeeding her baby, Che. A couple of glasses later we were laughing and exchanging banter like four old friends. We were all obviously excited and feeling pretty good about ourselves. Even Lisa, who I feared would be a dragon lady, turned out to be warm, funny and engaging. Libbi was more serious than I expected, with a quick wit and the great sense of humour that had been prominent in her previous work. I liked her immediately. Zoe was also warm and funny and I thought together we would make an interesting team.

The mood sobered slightly when we were told it was time to meet Eddie McGuire. I had done some last-minute research on Eddie because, never having followed sporting programs or quiz shows, I had only a vague idea who he was. I recalled reading in the media pages that he had been appointed CEO of the network some time back, but gave it scant thought. My son Aaron, who plays AFL and knew all about Eddie's passion for the Collingwood Football Club, gave me a quick background briefing, which was a lifesaver.

We were ushered to the inner sanctum of his office and were immediately put at ease. A man of considerable charm, Eddie is the sort who can mix it with anyone from Australia's richest and most powerful (including the Packers) to the most rabid footy fan. And even women, as I soon discovered. He enthused about his hopes for the program, and gave us some tips on how to avoid talking over the top of each other when debating issues on the panel, gleaned from his years in broadcasting.

For some reason I felt a need to strike a blow for those of us for whom sport is not the meaning of life. I suggested to Eddie that I didn't regard sport as news, that it irritated me to see sport constantly on the front page of the newspaper, and not on the back page where I felt it belonged. I was rather foolishly waving a red rag at a bull, but that's my way. He disagreed, but charmingly so. The others looked at me askance. Why was I baiting the boss? I suppose I just wanted to make it plain where I was coming from, and what he could expect of me on the show.

The morning of the third day, the screen test, we were given a makeover bright and early by the make-up artists and hairdressers. It was fun being transformed into glamour queens – little did I realise how I would eventually come to resent being imprisoned in the make-up chair for two hours every morning.

We talked through the topics we would debate before the cameras. I was disturbed that most of our discussion topics revolved around celebrities. Mia and Tara took the view that the broader issues facing women at home could best be tackled through this window. If some famous actress was having weight-loss difficulties or marital problems or addiction issues or psychological problems, we could thrash it out by using the celebrity as a 'hook'.

I couldn't imagine how some of the vacuous American bimbos depicted in women's magazines were significant or relevant to the more grounded and intelligent audience I hoped would watch our show. But I also felt I was on thin ice, since I really had no idea who any of these celebrities were, or what they had done. How could I talk confidently about people I had never even heard of?

We were introduced to a good-looking young man who was to be our link to this celebrity gossip. Mia was very excited when she told us that Pete Timms was to have a regular spot on the show. Zoe and Lisa gasped with apparent delight, Libbi looked bemused, and I sat looking blank. It turned out he had been a finalist on the original season of *Big Brother*, had gone on to become a minor celebrity in the gossip columns, and was now working for *Woman's Day* magazine. I tried desperately to look enthusiastic.

All made-up and ready to record the screen test, I dashed into the Channel 9 loos for a nervous pee, and realised Libbi was in the next cubicle.

'How long do you think we'll last?' she asked.

'A week, a month, who knows?' I responded. We giggled. It would be a great adventure, if nothing else. It was our running joke for the next five months. 'Still here!' we'd laugh disbelievingly.

The day we shot the screen test I was uncomfortable with the subject matter chosen for debate. Libbi and I had both suggested various political issues that could be debated, but the view from the production side was that politics was generally a turn-off. It was deemed boring for women at home. We had a half-hearted attempt at discussing the coup in Fiji, which was plastered all over the front pages that day, but none of us knew very much about what was going on in Suva, and there was certainly no time for research to help us discuss it. It worked against our push for more serious content.

In the end we talked about fashion, discussing how men and women have a different view about what clothes make a woman look good (I had no view on this) and the drug habit of some rock star whose name was totally unfamiliar to me.

After the screen test I emailed Libbi:

For me it was a struggle to think of much to say about any of the topics – it was over before it began. It felt like a lot of 30-second grabs – not a proper conversation.

Anyway, when I got home I just sat on the floor and cuddled Isabella (sprung from hospital this afternoon) and remembered that real life is more important than the superficial stuff of women's magazines.

She responded :

I know – it was all a little light on, though in terms of chemistry I thought we were comfy (or at least getting there). Life is more than women's magazines, though great editors know how to tell important stories through the peephole of someone's life.

I wonder if we will get the chance?

And will we get the chance all together?

Anyway. It was fun to trot round the paddock and lovely to meet you. It did feel better for you than last time, didn't it? It's such an emotional rollercoaster, this business.

With the show's future in the lap of the gods, I negotiated a period in which to disappear. I felt an urgent need to spend time with my older sister, Margaret, especially if I was soon to be tied down by a twelve-month contract. David and the family agreed that I should spend Christmas away from home – the first time I had ever done so – and with mixed feelings about what the following year might bring, I jumped on a plane bound for Canada, where my sister and brother-in-law live.

9

Since 2005 the amount of time I can spare for my village house in France has been greatly reduced, because I have a new priority and a new destination in my life. Every year, several times if I can manage it, I travel to beautiful Vancouver Island off the coast of British Columbia, where Margaret and her husband, Ken, have a farm.

My sister and I were separated for more than five decades, and reconnected by chance after my first memoir, *Au Revoir*, was published. During an interview on ABC's *Life Matters* on Radio National, Geraldine Doogue questioned me about this aspect of my story; I told her that I knew Margaret was in Canada, and worked at a university, but I had been unable to track her down. Later that day a former colleague of Margaret's contacted the radio station to say that she knew my sister and had a current address for her. When that call came through, I sat at my desk and sobbed for half an hour, shaking all over.

I can't really explain why finding Margaret was so important to me. Thousands of people have estranged siblings – especially half-brothers and -sisters – and they don't necessarily feel this intense desire to reunite. But I had always known that Margaret was a vital piece in the jigsaw of my life, and that I had genuinely missed her when she left home even though I was little more than a toddler at the time. My mother had always talked about Margaret during my childhood – there were lots of lovely black and white photographs of her growing up – and she also told me that Margaret had spent a lot of time looking after me when I was a baby. I have a hazy memory of sitting on a potty in the bathroom, peering into a small round hole in the tiles surrounding the bathtub. The story goes that Margaret told me a large tiger lived under the bath and that thought must have stayed with me for years, long after she left.

My husband and our children knew that I was determined to find Margaret some day, to talk through all those memories, both good and bad. When I found her again, it seemed I finally had my chance. When I wrote to Margaret, and sent her a copy of my book, she wrote back immediately. It was a brief note saying how delighted she was to have received my letter, and that she had started to read the book but that she found the early chapters about our childhood difficulties quite painful. She promised to write again soon, but there was nothing more. Complete silence for months and months. I was convinced that she had changed her mind and decided that she didn't really want to meet the little sister who would remind her of aspects of her life she had obviously effectively expunged from her memory.

Then a letter arrived. A long, warm and fascinating account of her life over the decades between her eighteenth birthday and the current day. She was about to turn sixty-eight. She apologised for the delay in getting back to me. She had somehow lost my original letter with my contact details.

'*I put your letter and book away in a safe place,*' she wrote. '*Guess what? I forgot where that was. I finally found it two days ago. I had put it with some art supplies in a very conspicuous place. Hmph! I'm afraid I have blindness of the mind.*'

I was so relieved to get her letter at last that it didn't occur to me that there was anything ominous in her words. I lose things all the time.

Put them 'somewhere safe' and then can't for the life of me remember where they are. I search until I find them. But I later found out it had been more than a case of misplacing – Margaret had actually forgotten that the book and letter even existed.

Towards the end of that first precious letter she wrote about her love of travelling to France (just one of the many things we later found that we had in common).

'*Our biggest problem now is getting there and back,*' she wrote. '*Unfortunately Ken and I are reaching that "where did I leave my keys?" stage. I find myself forgetting to turn the stove off, or pay some bills on time, and these little episodes are on the increase.*'

All the signs were there, I just didn't read them.

Margaret knew only too well that her memory was failing. She confided in Ken that she was worried about how forgetful she had become of late, and he strongly advised her to report her concerns to her doctor. Yet each time she made a routine visit she naturally forgot to mention her increasing confusion and forgetfulness. When she finally did talk to the doctor he said it was normal for her age. At that time she would have been in her mid-sixties.

So she did what most people do in this situation. She covered for herself by developing strategies to disguise the fact that she was increasingly unable to remember the names of her close friends and family, that she constantly lost things and was finding it difficult to remember even the most simple routines. She could still function at a level that convinced everyone, including herself, that nothing was wrong. She was just getting a little older and a little forgetful. Nothing more.

Eventually, Ken cajoled Margaret into seeking a referral to a neurologist. She wasn't just forgetting where she put the car keys; she was actually hiding them. The mail started to go astray. She would forget to pass on phone messages and she also started to become unsettled and at times agitated. She stopped reading and watching television and started to go to bed earlier and earlier. Losing herself in sleep. It was totally uncharacteristic of this vibrant, involved woman.

Every Wednesday, Margaret had lunch with her art group, a small, tight-knit band of women from vastly different backgrounds who loved the pleasure of getting together, painting, and then sitting down to a meal, each bringing a plate of food to share. For nearly twenty years they had met in each other's homes. They would spread plastic sheets on the tables, and sit around talking and laughing non-stop while painting furiously. Members of the group had also travelled overseas together, packing up their oils and watercolours and renting small houses in the French, Spanish or Italian countryside.

One such trip – this time to France – had been planned several months after Margaret had her appointment with the neurologist. The results of the test had not been good, and Ken was keeping it close to his chest on the assumption that Margaret wouldn't want people to know. It was a definite diagnosis of Alzheimer's and, according to the test results, her condition was fairly advanced. By no means was she in the 'early stages' of her long and tortuous journey. She had already negotiated a big stretch of the road, and she had done so without her condition being detected by her doctor or her friends. It was obvious that her intelligence had enabled her to bluff her way through. By the time her condition was finally acknowledged she had already reached the stage of retreating into her own world.

Ken and Margaret and two friends rented a holiday house in a coastal town north of Bordeaux. I was in Paris, at the end of my annual French walking tour, and took a train down to spend a day with them. It had been almost a year since our first overwhelming reunion and I was keen to maintain contact as much as possible. They met me at the station and took me to their little house where a wonderful lunch was waiting. I didn't notice anything different about Margaret, except perhaps that she looked a little thinner and frailer than I remembered. I had thought of her as being small but wiry and strong. This time she seemed a little less confident in her stride, more cautious, more hesitant.

After lunch we went sightseeing, and stopped for a cup of tea in a local cafe. Margaret and her friend Dorothy left to do some window-shopping, then Ken put his hand on my arm and told me, quickly and quietly, that Margaret had been diagnosed with Alzheimer's disease. I was devastated. How could this be? My clever sister. I'd only just found her again. I had only just started to rebuild our relationship. And now I was going to lose her.

I cried on the train going back to Paris that night. Selfish tears of pain and loss. I wasn't thinking of Margaret but of myself, and my anguish. I was angry and felt cheated. It wasn't meant to be like this. Our reunion was supposed to have a happy ending, not be the beginning of a nightmare.

My reaction was one of grief, understandable at the time. But after wrestling with my emotions for a few days, I recognised the truth of the situation. How fortunate I had been to find Margaret when I did. How lucky I was to have enjoyed the time we had already shared over the previous eighteen months, writing and talking and reminiscing about our common heritage. Imagine if I had found Margaret five years hence? Then, perhaps, I would have good cause to feel sorry – for both of us. I had to put it into perspective. Finding Margaret had been totally positive. A gift in my life. Nothing, not even this tragic development, could spoil it now.

10

The Christmas I spent in Canada in 2006 was my first in a cold climate, and it was tremendous fun. We cut a perfect tree from the local Christmas-tree farm, and decorated it with great care. More than twelve of Ken's relatives were invited for dinner, and everything was organised down to the last bonbon. In Australia, the Christmas feast is traditionally served at lunch, but here in Canada it was an early evening meal of roast turkey with all the trimmings. It was icy cold outside, not snowing, but hovering below zero. There were fires in the two living rooms and the house – like all houses in Canada – is centrally heated and therefore comfortable all year round. The meal seemed more appropriate to this climate than to ours at home, where I am usually sweating over a wood stove on Christmas day with temperatures well over the 30-degree mark.

It was more than eighteen months since Margaret's original diagnosis, and even though I had seen her since, when she and Ken had come to Australia for a couple of months to reconnect with brothers Jon and Dan, I was shocked by her deterioration. My sister could put on a show of being totally with it, but in reality she had trouble managing even the most simple tasks, and putting names to faces was almost impossible for her. She was able to help me prepare vegetables for dinner, and she could still do the washing up efficiently, but using the stove and coordinating a meal was completely beyond her. She had lost quite a bit of weight and I had trouble convincing her to eat – for breakfast all she would consider was a single kiwifruit and a cup of green tea. Her lack of appetite affected her energy levels and made her appear delicate.

The most distressing aspect was that she appeared totally lost and confused a lot of the time. She was restless, unable to remain seated for more than a few moments, and spent a lot of time gazing out of the windows or standing in front of the wall calendar in the kitchen trying to work out what day of the week it was. Ken used the calendar as a way of keeping her in touch with appointments and engagements, and she would stare at it constantly, pointing to each day and asking about entries that had been written in. Every half-hour she would return to the calendar as though she was using it to cling desperately to keep a grip on the real world. Margaret's short-term memory had faded to such an extent that if she answered the phone and took a message for Ken, she would forget who had called within two seconds of hanging up. As this failure made her very anxious I put a pen and paper next to the phone, and made sure it remained there; that way she could write the message down as it was being given to her. She also became obsessed with the family's cats, Boris and Sheba, and followed their movements in and out of the house very closely. They enjoyed this attention, because she kept feeding them – filling their bowls ten or fifteen times a day because she simply couldn't remember that she had already done so.

My sister had also taken to hiding things and moving objects from one place to another. She was someone who had always been busy, on the go. Now she couldn't think of any constructive way of filling her time so instead she relentlessly picked up any item that was left lying around and put it somewhere else. The cups from afternoon tea were put in the oven, slippers left lying in the family room were put in a drawer, and mail collected from the letterbox turned up in the freezer.

Ken had to hide things that he really needed, such as car and house keys and incoming bills. It was all very frustrating.

However, Margaret loved accompanying me on long walks, and these provided a great opportunity for us to talk about the past and discuss the different and yet similar paths that our separate lives had taken. Her memory of many of the events of her childhood had disappeared, but she retained the ability to laugh at some of the grim stories she shared with me. Her sense of humour remained intact.

I planned to leave Canada immediately after Christmas to spend three weeks in France before returning home to start work on *The Catch-Up*. Two days before I left Canada, Ken became quite ill. He was dizzy and short of breath, and appeared exhausted. I was not surprised. Caring for Margaret was more than a full-time job and it was beginning to take its toll. I started to panic about leaving them. How would he cope if he wasn't well himself? How would he manage meals, and getting Margaret into the shower, and having to do all the shopping and day-to-day organising without help?

Frantic, I rang a close family member and expressed my concerns. He rallied immediately, and within hours a homecare agency had been contacted. Although Ken had previously resisted the idea of outside help, it now became imperative. By the time I departed a roster of carers had been drawn up and Ken admitted for the first time that he simply could no longer manage the situation alone.

I left for France with a heavy heart. It was bitterly cold in Vancouver when I boarded the plane there, and freezing in Paris when I arrived half a day later. January is not an ideal month to visit Frayssinet because my small village house lacks central heating; however, the walls are very thick and I have installed a new wood stove which makes conditions comfortable even in the depths of winter. I burn large oak logs bought from a neighbouring farmer, and while they don't last as long or burn as hot as Australian hardwood they keep the house cosy overnight. I have also hung heavy, well-lined curtains, which help to muffle draughts from the ancient windows that no longer fit snugly. Over time the stone front wall has dropped in places, and the windows and doors are out of kilter. It would take major renovation and great expense to repair or replace them. In any event I love the look of the old frames and the original glass that has a distinctive watery appearance.

Apart from my emotional desire to spend time in France, the practical reason for this visit was to carry out the stills photography for the French chapter of *The Long Table*, a cookbook I was contracted to write. If the television show indeed went ahead and was a success, I didn't know when and how I would get away to complete this vital part of the project. I wanted shots taken of the markets and the local region, of my friends and neighbours, and of my kitchen, to illustrate my story of learning the French way of shopping and cooking. I had arranged for my talented French photographer friend, Nadja, who lives in Normandy, to come down for a week so we could collaborate on the pictures.

But despite the fact I had a genuine reason to go to France, David was not thrilled at my decision to run away yet again, especially when I was facing a critically busy year in which work would often keep us apart. My visits to Frayssinet continue to be a huge source of conflict between us. I am torn by my need to spend time in my little house and by the knowledge that David is unhappy whenever I am staying there. It represents a period in my life that, although often difficult and sad, made a great impression on me. It's as though that dash for freedom from my marriage and responsibilities has taught me a lot about myself; every time I go back I reconnect with France, yet the fact that I am so far from home and living in a foreign culture also reminds me that my priorities ultimately lie with my family in Australia.

I also know that the house in Frayssinet is a refuge, a retreat from the hectic pace and expectations of my normal life. I can close the doors and shutters and be alone, or swing them open and have a party. I love driving my beat-up old Peugeot, zipping along the winding lanes, through the woods and villages, and I love the sense of independence I feel living there. Being in France always recharges my batteries, and after my visit to Canada I believed it would put me in a good frame of mind for the work that lay ahead during 2007. I decided to put the TV show out of my head completely, remembering what had happened last time I left Australia expecting to return to a relatively well-paid job. In a sense, when I am living in the village it's as though I have completely escaped from my real life into another world; a fantasy world.

My initial trip to France back in 2000 was like falling in love for the first time. I saw the entire experience through rose-coloured glasses, just as one looks at a lover and sees nothing but beauty and goodness. My perspective has greatly modified these last few years, not just because of the everyday changes among the people I am close to when I am staying in my little house, but also because of essential changes within myself. I am just not the same woman who ran away from home at fifty. I used to fantasise about moving there permanently, and only the thought of abandoning my grandchildren made the idea impossible; I would miss them too much. Now I can see that I would probably go crazy if I lived in France all year round, because of the language barrier and the social difference among the expat community.

Making friends has never been a problem for me, but with hindsight I realise that I would have been wiser to include more non-English-speaking French people in my social circle. I hadn't studied French at school, so it was natural for me to gravitate towards English speakers, but it was also rather lazy. I feel very timid about speaking bad French when, in fact, speaking lots of bad French and struggling to understand and to be understood would have forced me to grasp the language with confidence. I have discovered that when I have to buy a train ticket or transact some business at the post office I can muddle along in French quite well. Gradually my ear has adjusted so that I can follow French conversations if they are not spoken too rapidly. But once I'm socialising in the company of bilingual friends I become self-conscious

and tongue-tied, and resist speaking French for fear of making a total
fool of myself. This has seriously limited my ability to get to know the
locals better.

There are many native English speakers living permanently in
France who simply don't bother learning the language, beyond basic
words and phrases which enable them to get by in restaurants and at
the market. This effectively disconnects them from the local community,
because they can't interact socially. Dinner parties become purely
English-speaking affairs, and they cling to each other rather than
trying to assimilate. This is not the way I want to experience France. It's
frustrating not being able to crack a joke, or to join some of the lively
debates on politics which are a feature of conversation at any French
dinner table.

After my first six-month stay in France, living in a room behind a
shop in a medieval village, my return visits have been shorter, usually
six to eight weeks at most. Every time I get to the point of beginning
to feel I am making some progress in communicating, I pack up and
return to Australia, where most of my newly acquired language skills
are quickly forgotten. Work, family and farm take priority. I am also
not very disciplined when it comes to studying. I get fits of enthusiasm
then it all falls by the wayside. I realise that unless I experience 'full
French immersion' by living with a totally non-English-speaking family
for three months at least then I will never become 'almost French'.

I have also discovered that life in small communities has its social ups
and downs, especially among the expat community, and my village is no
exception. Among the small number of hamlets which surround it are
a wide variety of people from vastly different backgrounds, and there
have been rivalries and jealousies, mental illness, nervous breakdowns,
alcoholic collapses, horrific car accidents, deaths from cancer and
heart attacks, stand-up fights, affairs, marriage break-ups and plenty of
acrimony. The population is ageing – both the French and the expats
– and this has brought problems too; health and financial problems

mainly. I was oblivious to all of this during my first visits to France, but it has become increasingly obvious, and keeping clear of it has proven extremely difficult. As a part-time resident I drift in and out and that makes it tricky to keep up with the local politics. If there has been a falling out – and these seem to happen quite a lot – I'm usually unaware and, quite frankly, I don't really want to get involved. I just wish they'd all get over it and get along together.

Since I first bought my house nearly eight years ago, two more cottages in the village have been bought by Australians aspiring to live there part of each year. They are just around the corner from me. I know and like them – they are friends of my old mate Jock – yet curiously we have rarely been 'in residence' at the same time. There have been plenty of Kangaroo Valley jokes of course, and the locals now call the main street Rue de Billabong because it backs onto a bubbling stream. However the Australian influx is nothing compared with the English invasion. New houses – not very attractive new houses – are being built on the outskirts of the village, and they appear to be predominantly for Britons looking to make their home in the region. Because of its distance from the Channel, the Lot was relatively free from tourism and immigration for many years. Slowly and steadily, however, the population has been changing, and this has to some extent changed the character of the villages.

Those English who do speak French fluently have a pretty fair idea of the local reaction because there are mumblings in the bar and an undercurrent, among the older population, about *les Anglaises*. On the surface the local businesspeople appear delighted with the relatively affluent new population because without that cash flow their shops and restaurants would undoubtedly have difficulty surviving.

Like all migrant populations, the newcomers tend to cluster together for companionship. In one local restaurant there is a large gathering every Wednesday night, with a floating population of between eight and fifteen English-speaking locals. It can get quite wild and woolly in there as they talk and laugh loudly while eating pizza and gulping the local cheap red wine. They often finish with round after round of Irish coffee or strong liqueurs like Armagnac or Grand Marnier. Individually, they are all very lovable people, but en masse they can be quite daunting. I have joined them quite a few times but don't feel totally comfortable in their midst. I can't quite put my finger on it.

The locals I have come to know remain as delightful as ever. My neighbour Madame Thomas always stops for a chat on her way to the *boulangerie*, and Christian and Christianne, who run the corner bar and the small cafe at the lake, always welcome me with open arms. I feel totally comfortable when I am living in my little house, but I'm aware that no matter how hard I might try, I will always be a foreigner. I remain *étrange* – strange – to the people here. I'm a married woman who comes to her house but doesn't bring her husband. I'm an author who has written a book about a local restaurant and also made a documentary on the same subject (which few of them have seen). Yet I don't drive a flashy car or live in a chateau, which I think is also viewed with some curiosity. *Ton Ton* Raymond (Uncle Raymond), one of the characters in my documentary about Madame Murat's restaurant, expressed dismay that I was living in such a modest cottage, slap bang on the main road, in the middle of my rather down-at-heel village. I fear he pictured me in some charming *grande maison* in an idyllic pastoral setting. *Ton Ton* didn't understand that, for me, even the most modest cottage in France was a grand extravagance that I could only maintain by working very, very hard. I have such a different attitude to these things than my husband. He's much more inclined to work towards squirrelling resources away for a rainy day, but I need to live my life and enjoy the fruits of my labours. France is an extravagance that I can barely justify but I will continue to try to make it work so that I can keep dipping my toe into my other life, even if only for a few weeks at a time.

11

Second time lucky. I returned home from France to find that, this time, the TV show was definitely going ahead. We were each appointed our own personal producer as a minder, and a fashion stylist was commissioned – style was going to be a vital element of the show. Back at the farm I was getting organised – dashing around trying to get the garden in order – in preparation for being away from home five days a week. The producers found me a small apartment in Milsons Point, just under the Harbour Bridge.

There were constant calls on our time from the production office. My producer, Cathy, and the stylist, Talia, together with a cameraman and sound recordist, came up to the farm for a day to 'look through my wardrobe' and to shoot a quick 'snapshot of my life' that would be screened during our first week to air – to give the audience a bit of an idea about who I was, where I lived, my personality. The other cast members were put through the same experience.

The following week I was asked to fly to Sydney to have my eyebrows plucked by Nathan, who was described as 'the eyebrow whisperer'. By now the process was beginning to feel a bit weird to me. Not only had a film crew been sticking a camera inside my disorganised walk-in wardrobe, with the stylist poring over my skirts, blouses and shoes, but now my eyebrows were about to be given a makeover. I have indistinct blonde eyebrows and lashes, and have never, ever attacked them with a pair of tweezers. I was assured it was essential to achieve 'the look' that was required. Bemused, then seduced, I surrendered.

We were primped and preened. Our faces were exfoliated with a beauty treatment called 'dermabrasion'; our hair was coloured, cut and styled; we were given underwear to pull in our tummies, and stockings, shoes and fantastic accessories. We were assigned not one but two make-up artists to transform us into daytime TV stars. It was totally unreal, but in some ways also a lot of fun. I was asked to ditch my glasses and use contact lenses, which I knew would be problematic. It also seemed a bit of a contradiction, as we were constantly encouraged to 'be ourselves' as much as possible and I had been wearing glasses for nearly twenty years.

For many women, I imagine the whole experience would be a dream come true. Having expensive new clothes to try on, being treated to a new hairstyle and professional make-up. Being pampered. These beauty sessions were aimed at making us feel special, but they also gave us a chance to get to know each other a little and to develop, rather desperately, like a group of speed-daters, some sort of chemistry that might later translate onto a TV screen for our prospective audience. Bonding, we were told, was essential.

We performed a full-day photo shoot in dozens of different outfits. One minute all in black, next all in white, then in bold primary colours. We shot promotional videos which would run as ads to promote the show and also in the opening credits for the program, dancing, twirling, laughing, uttering throwaway lines that would be then edited together to produce a glossy, pacy introduction.

We spent a week in Sydney rehearsing. Instead of throwing us cold to the audience on day one, it was wisely decided to warm us up by doing some live pilots, complete with interview guests and direct crosses to Pete Timms in the *Woman's Day* office.

Once again my indifference to celebrity gossip reared its head. I had vaguely heard of Britney Spears but I had no idea who she was, or what she was supposed to be famous for. When Anna Nicole Smith died just before our first show went to air, I had to admit to my fellow cast members in a production meeting that I had never even heard of the woman. I had *no* idea. I figured I would just have to button up during these discussions or somehow bluff my way through.

We all had vastly different areas of interest, which should have been a plus. Libbi had broad areas of knowledge and experience, from music and show business to politics and women's issues, and even sport (another blind spot for me). Lisa was also very up on current affairs, sport and politics, which was a particular passion. She sometimes stunned me with her detailed knowledge. Zoe was obviously very bright but she had made a conscious decision at some point in her life that news – real news – was upsetting and depressing. She avoided the evening TV news programs, and never looked at a newspaper apart from reading her stars and the celebrity gossip. As a result she didn't know the names or faces of many local or international politicians and had no idea about the issues I believed were important to our audience.

Before our rehearsal period we were thrown into a publicity tour – Sydney, Melbourne, Brisbane – to introduce us to the media. We were not briefed about how we should behave during these interviews, but were encouraged yet again to 'be ourselves'. We *were* the show. Our individual personalities were the key to it all, our minders at Nine constantly reminded us.

The interview we did with *Woman's Day* was a shocker. The magazine was a sponsor of the program, and proposed running a full-page feature article every week. We were taken to a restaurant overlooking the ocean at Bondi, subjected to more 'glam' photographs, and then invited to lunch with the magazine's journalist. She was obviously keen for an 'off the wall' story and she got it. After two glasses of wine Lisa was in full flight, throwing around quick responses and funny one-liners. I suppose we were lulled into a false sense of security because the magazine was involved with the program. I assumed they would do a favourable 'advertorial'. Not so. Instead, they chose to publish some embarrassing banter between Lisa and me. What might have seemed funny at the time didn't appear quite so amusing in print. Our publicist was starting to look very nervous.

There was something about Lisa that was hard to fathom. She was such an intelligent, humorous and beautiful woman. Yet from the beginning she acted out some strange and unpredictable behaviour. She would vomit at the slightest provocation. The first time was in the boardroom when we were delivered coffee, tea and hot chocolate by Mia's assistant, carried from the canteen in paper cups with lids. She sipped her drink, then let out a shriek and ran from the room, retching into her hand. By mistake, she had been given coffee instead of hot chocolate. It seemed she didn't like coffee, or had some violent allergic reaction to it. This episode was the first of many similar puzzling dramas.

We were taken aside one by one and asked to 'keep an eye on Lisa'. Libbi, in particular, was charged with the role of being Lisa's minder, and I am quite convinced this caused tension between them.

Sometimes I'd feel like pinching myself, as a jolt back to reality. It was an extraordinary opportunity, falling into the world of live daytime television, but so much of what went on was bizarre and false. I sensed it was nothing more than an illusion.

12

'The Secret reveals the most powerful law in the universe. The knowledge of this law has run like a golden thread through the lives and the teachings of all the prophets, seers, sages and saviours in the world's history, and through the lives of all truly great men and women. All they have ever accomplished or attained has been done in full accordance with this most powerful law.'

—Rhonda Byrne, *The Secret*.

A week before our show was scheduled to go to air Mia Freedman handed me an unmarked DVD.

'Do you know about The Secret?' she asked.

'What secret?' I replied, trying not to look totally stupid.

'I want you to watch this DVD. It's amazing. It's the reason we are doing this show. You'll understand when you see it – Tara and I totally believe in it.'

I stuck the disc in my bag and caught the plane back to the farm for the weekend. I had family visiting, and lots of lunches and dinners to cook, and it was late on Sunday afternoon before I suddenly remembered the disc and pushed it into the DVD player.

After fifteen minutes I called out to David: 'I think I'm in trouble here. Come and look at this. Mia and Tara think this is for real – they believe in it. I think I'm heading for big trouble.'

David sat with me for a few minutes and watched the film. We were in agreement that it was a load of new-age rubbish and totally implausible, but he advised me just to ignore it and get on with the job. He could see no point in making a fuss about something he perceived as being 'silly and trivial'. I couldn't help feeling that it was a bit more worrying.

The Secret began life as a self-help video and became an international success in March 2006 with a book, a CD, and a desk calendar. The creation of an Australian TV producer, Rhonda Byrne, it is based on a theory known as 'the law of attraction' or 'like attracts like'. According to Byrne, each individual has the potential to become wealthy and successful – it's just a matter of 'asking the universe to provide'. The mantra is Ask. Believe. Receive. When Oprah Winfrey featured The Secret on her television show, she interviewed people who believed that it had changed their lives. They claimed they had gone from being poor and frustrated to becoming rich and successful simply by imagining they *were* rich and successful. The book includes the story of a man who was sick of getting bills that he couldn't afford to pay, so he took his bank statement and whited out the total, then wrote in a new total and 'visualised' that he had a large sum of money in his account. He claimed that within a month cheques just started arriving into his account and his financial problems were solved.

Some people might simply laugh at such nonsense, but to me it seemed dangerous. Wacky theories such as these prey on the vulnerability of unhappy people, leading them to believe that they can easily live their dreams. The only people getting rich, in my opinion, are the people writing, publishing and promoting such ideas. I was mortified to think that these intelligent, well-educated and sophisticated women who were my new colleagues could possibly fall for such obvious nonsense.

The following week Mia bounced into the production office and touched my arm.

'Did you watch the DVD?' she asked. 'What did you think?'

'I thought it was the greatest load of claptrap I've ever seen,' I responded. 'I don't believe a word of it.'

Mia looked hurt and went very quiet. I felt awful for bursting her bubble, but I just couldn't pretend to go along with the whole thing. Apparently Zoe had seen the film and was also convinced it was life-changing information. I wasn't sure about Libbi and Lisa, but I knew that I couldn't support the notion that The Secret was the reason behind our show getting the nod of approval from the network. I also sensed that the concept could be introduced as a topic of discussion on the program, and I wanted to distance myself from it from the word go.

Later that week I was in the production office, reading press clippings on the corkboard. Articles that had been published in advance of the show were displayed for us all to see. There was also a curious media release that talked about *The Catch-Up* as though it had been running for several months. It spoke of the show being a 'huge ratings success' for the Nine Network, and of the prospect of moving it from its daytime slot to prime time in the evening. I was totally nonplussed. Then I realised what was going on. Someone in the office had written the release in an attempt to send out positive messages to 'the universe' that the show was going to be a runaway success story. It was going to make us all rich and famous. We were living The Secret.

I didn't know whether to laugh or cry.

13

No matter how crazy things got at Channel 9, or the suspended reality we lived in at the studio, outside events could be relied upon to bring me crashing back to earth with a thud.

Our children and their partners had supported both me and David through the difficult period of our marriage. They listened patiently to us both, to our rantings and ravings, our tears and irrational outpourings. Naturally, they became angry and frustrated with both of us at various times, yet they were understanding, long-suffering and forgiving. Given the stoutness of their support, how could we have foreseen that not long after David and I agreed to resolve our differences, to make up and move on, the relationships closest to our hearts would begin to crumble?

First it was Lorna and Aaron. I knew they had been experiencing difficulties but in my typical head-in-the-sand fashion I just assumed they would work it out. They always seemed happy when they brought the children to the farm, and even though I could sense tension between them at times I just assumed that they would hang in there. They had built a beautiful home together and established a lovely garden, and they were both working hard for their future and the future of their children.

From time to time Lorna had made comments to me about frustrations in her relationship with Aaron, but in reality she had protected me from her true feelings. Lorna is a brave young woman. She wasn't happy and she left. I was horrified. I didn't beg or plead but I desperately wanted her to go back to our son. To work it through. To resolve the problems. Aaron was a wreck. He fell apart and we did our best to pick up the pieces. He wasn't facing reality either, although he acknowledged a lot of the responsibility for what had gone wrong in their marriage. I kept reminding myself that they had been very young when they got together, and that the situation wasn't black and white. Like all relationships, the problems were complex and both partners had made mistakes along the way. During the period of their break-up, there was a lot of anger and some truly heart-breaking moments. I kept hoping for a happy resolution, thinking that perhaps in time things might settle down. I was deluding myself.

What about the children? They were unhappy and confused, and I believe to this day that they would love their parents to be together again. That's pretty normal, I suppose. We see a lot of them – they come to the farm with their father and they also visit us with Lorna. At first I tried to talk to them about what had happened, but it all seemed too sad to talk about and Ella, in particular, could not articulate her feelings very well. All I can say is that they are well-loved, happy children who see a lot of both their parents and seem to have come to terms with the situation. It wasn't always so, but over time, Lorna and Aaron have reached a comfortable place in their relationship and often socialise together, with the children. That's a very good thing. But it doesn't stop me from still feeling the pain of it all. I can't even begin to imagine how terrible it must be for grandparents when there is a marriage split and they are denied access to their grandchildren because of custody battles or financial disputes.

Aaron and Lorna's split came as a rude shock to me, and this has been a common thread through all my dealings with my children and their partners. There is a tendency within the family to shelter me from anything that is negative or painful or unhappy. To protect me from the harsh realities of life. They know I love everyone to be happy. No conflict. No confrontation. The past few years when David and I almost separated – 'the troubles', as I now jokingly refer to them – were an aberration. Until this rocky period I had always sought to keep things running smoothly. From the moment I first set up house with David, this is how I wanted things to be.

So when Miriam phoned us from Adelaide in early 2007 to say that she and Rick had separated, I could barely believe the words searing down the line. She was crying, of course, and was in profound shock herself. It had been sudden, turbulent and, she felt certain, quite final. At the time, Ethan and Lynne and their children were still living with us at the farm. Ethan was at work. I don't know where David was – maybe at the gym. I reeled from my office to the kitchen where Lynne was setting up a feed for Isabella. I blurted out the bare facts and she, too, howled in disbelief. We sat at the table, sobbing and drinking tea and trying to put the fragments of information we had together. Dismay and disbelief were the overriding emotions.

Initially Miriam wanted to 'come home'. To pack up the house and the four boys and run back to an emotionally safe place. I readily agreed, feeling a need not only to see her but to help out in some way. That plan only lasted a few hours. By then the troops – Miriam's solid core of strong and supportive female friends – had rallied. They buoyed her spirits and provided plenty of practical as well as emotional support.

One of the first things I did was to send an SMS message to Rick, who was staying with a friend temporarily. Just to let him know that no matter what had happened between him and Miriam, we loved and supported him too. We did. We had always loved Rick, and I was well aware that he would be hurting just as much as our daughter. He decided to take some leave from work and visit his father in Sydney. It was only a few weeks after the initial bust-up, and he asked if he could stay overnight with us at the farm on the way through. Of course he could; it would be good to see him and to talk.

In the meantime, I spoke with Miriam virtually every day. Her mood changed constantly. She swung from feeling happy and relieved that she was free from what she saw as an untenable situation, to feeling frightened and lonely and desperately sad at how it had all ended.

As usual I kept hoping that there might be a resolution. They could have marriage counselling perhaps. They could give it a second chance, as David and I had done. My continued denial of the truth of the situation and my blind optimism that that there could be a reconciliation were galling for Miriam. What she wanted and needed from me was unequivocal love and support for the very difficult decision she had made. She had my love, but she knew that at heart I wanted her to change her mind. To capitulate and compromise.

In the end she became angry with my attitude, and I can't really blame her. It was the first time in thirty-four years that she had been so critical of me, and I was shocked and hurt. As an outside observer of her marriage I had perceived various problems over the years, but had concluded that they were just the normal domestic ructions that all families experience. Miriam had always given me the impression that everything between her and Rick was good, and that their marriage was solid in spite of the flare-ups and clashes of personality. Because I wanted the marriage to be solid I chose to believe this implicitly. Because I wanted the marriage to survive I clung to the notion that maybe, just maybe, they could reconcile.

I flew to Adelaide to visit Miriam and the four boys. Miriam seemed very positive, very together, very upbeat. The boys were their usual boisterous selves. They are always delighted to see me and full of talk and noise and laughter. I took them out to lunch – I wanted to talk to them on their own to establish how they were coping with the situation. I broached the subject cautiously.

'How do you feel about Mummy and Daddy? About them not being together any more?'

Eamonn looked vaguely into the distance. Theo glanced at the menu. Gus wriggled and fidgeted and looked uncomfortable. It was Sam who was the spokesman, as usual.

'Well I was sad at first,' he said with a serious expression. 'But now I've got used to the idea and it's okay.'

So that was it. I burst into tears and the four boys huddled around me, patting my back and giving me hugs. My attempt to comfort them was a complete fiasco.

I realise now that my reactions to the marriage breakdown were more about how I felt, about my pain, about my dismay that my 'perfect' world had yet again taken a big knock. Of course I was desperately sad for both Miriam and Rick that it hadn't worked out the way they planned. They had been through so much together – they really were very young when they first met – and they had supported each other and worked hard together and it just seemed dismal for it all to end like that. So suddenly, like an axe falling.

In particular, I cherished the memories of the way they worked together at the births of their four boys. I was there for every birth. They took control and responsibility for everything – Eamonn, Sam and Theo were born at home with midwives and Miriam and Rick made a brilliant team. Rick swam with Miriam in the birthing pool and cradled her between his legs each time as she delivered their four large sons.

They cherished those memories too, and eventually I realised that nothing could ever negate those extraordinary moments of intimacy. They were the building blocks of their lives and, even though they were no longer together as a couple, they were united in their reverence for this chapter in their lives.

Positives sometimes emerge from negative situations. Both Miriam and Rick seem much happier now and, after the initial shock, grief and anger, they have settled into a really good relationship revolving around the boys. It seems to me that they have handled the fallout for their kids particularly well. Miriam notified the school counsellor immediately after the break-up so that their teachers could keep an eye on the boys and watch out for any signs of trauma. But there were no such signs. Their schoolwork didn't suffer. They didn't act out any adverse behaviour in the classroom or playground. I'm not suggesting that they were untouched or unaffected by what happened, I'm just saying that they appear to have taken it in their stride, and because their parents have a fundamentally respectful relationship, the boys are happy.

14

The Catch-Up went to air in February. The first week was terrifying. We had a studio audience, and had to march onto the set during the opening music and credits, sit up at the desk facing the cameras and start talking immediately. We had been wired up with microphones – always two, in case one malfunctioned – and we also had earpieces so that the producers in the control room could help direct the flow of the conversation. Libbi was against this idea, fearing it would interfere with the authenticity of our discussions, but in the end she relented.

My main problem with the show was always the content. I knew it was necessary to keep it broad and entertaining, but to me the topics we discussed were invariably too frivolous, too lightweight. I had plenty of opportunity to voice my opinion in the production meetings that preceded the show. Every morning we met with the creative crew to toss around ideas for that day's show. One of the problems was that the other girls, who all had quite long distances to drive, were sometimes late arriving to this meeting. We only had an hour to thrash around ideas and then we had to head to the dressing room for hair and make-up. Every day, it seemed, we had less and less time to make intelligent decisions about what issues we would deal with on the show.

From my perspective, there was definitely a dumbing-down factor. At first I had been told that we were aiming for an audience of intelligent career-minded women who were at home with young children, but I quickly realised we were aiming for the sort of audience who watch Dr Phil or American soaps. It was disappointing.

We were given a variety of guests to interview, as well as guest panellists who would join us for most of the show and also be involved in interviewing the other guests. We had Julia Gillard (we talked mostly about her hair and her boyfriend), Amanda Vanstone (we talked about her dinner parties) and Kathy Lette (we gave her new book a big plug). Nine wanted men on the panel from time to time, so we had Sam Newman from *The Footy Show* (I found him a very strange character) and Andrew Bolt, a right-wing newspaper columnist from Melbourne who didn't really know how to handle four prattling women. If they were the best 'blokes' in all Australia that we could entice onto the show, it raised some real questions.

Mia wanted controversy and Lisa did her best to create it. Pauline Hanson released a book in which she claimed she'd had an affair with David Oldfield. The minute the story hit the papers he was invited onto the show to give an emphatic denial – it was squirmingly embarrassing to see him being interviewed by a panel of women which included his wife, and Libbi's body language made it patently obvious she did not endorse the decision to bring him onto the show.

The desire to make 'news' led our inexperienced team down treacherous paths. We were given the gangland queen Judy Moran as a guest, but were not advised to avoid certain subjects because of a big court case running in Melbourne. She was a spine-chillingly scary woman – cold and intimidating – and I really would have been happy to sit out that particular interview. Not surprisingly, she made actionable statements – we were foolishly unaware. When it became apparent the next morning that the Nine Network was now in serious trouble with the Victorian judicial system, we were given an in-depth briefing by the station's lawyers. It was like closing the stable door after the horse had bolted.

A few weeks after we first went to air, it was decided that having all of us interviewing one guest at a time wasn't working very well. Our interviewing styles were vastly different, and I often felt I was struggling to get a question in. I think we all felt the same way at various times.

It was agreed we would put our hands up for those interviews that most interested us and that we would be split into pairs according to these preferences. Generally Libbi and I teamed up, as did Zoe and Lisa. This was a much better system from my perspective. Some of the guests we were given were absurd. There was a 'baby whisperer' who charged anxious parents a small fortune to stay overnight and teach their babies to sleep (it used to be called mothercraft). There were the identical twin sisters who talked in unison, answering each question in perfect synchronisation. There were various clairvoyants and psychics who were going to 'pick up on' various aspects of our personalities and do spontaneous 'readings' with the live audience. I have absolutely no patience with such nonsense. During the week of rehearsals we had interviewed a psychic and, while the cameras were rolling, she turned to me and started to pick up 'deep vibrations from my aura'. Those were her words. She said a few obvious things that she could easily have found out about in advance by reading my website or by googling me.

'I think what you're really picking up on is my deep cynicism,' I quipped, smiling sweetly.

It wasn't our job to make the talent look foolish, but I just couldn't help myself. It became a running joke in the production office that whenever there was a wacky guest Mary was 'out' of the interview. I was happy.

Libbi was considered to be difficult by some of the production team. She wasn't always easygoing, she often questioned decisions and argued with the producers if she didn't feel comfortable with what they were proposing – like taking a swing at Sam Newman as part of a judo segment, or participating in advertorials with scripted questions and answers for sponsors. During the mornings, while we prepared ourselves for the show, all the other girls would chain-smoke, dashing out the back door with their hair in rollers, half made-up, puffing like mad and making themselves, in my opinion, even more wound up and tense. Libbi hadn't smoked for years and took it up again, I guess because of the pressure we were under, and because Zoe and Lisa were smoking. She usually forgot to buy her own cigarettes and instead helped herself to the others' packets, which caused tension in the dressing room. Zoe started to hide her cigarettes and Libbi could be heard swearing while she searched for them. Next day Libbi would turn up with several packets of Zoe's favourite brand and everything would be fine until the cigarettes ran out again.

I tried to remain calm in the mornings and to set aside time for clear thinking and to gather my thoughts on the topics we had chosen (or that had been chosen for us) to discuss. As the anchor, Libbi endeavoured to create some structure within the program. She wanted the conversations between us to flow more naturally, and tried setting up 'links' that would enable us to jump from one topic to the next without it appearing clunky. It was a bit of an uphill battle – she was the only one who had any experience at making live television work, and her exasperation with the rest of us was often received as bad humour. I could see what she was trying to do, trying to pull it all together, but I don't think Lisa and Zoe or some of the production team had the same level of appreciation. When she fought for what she considered to be the best for the show, like insisting that the hairdryers be switched off while the cast had their final pre-show content briefing, she was not popular.

But apart from a few spats, I believe we all got along pretty well despite the craziness of our situation. We laughed a lot, and our mornings together having our hair and make-up done were often hilarious – undoubtedly more entertaining than the show itself. In spite of everything I genuinely liked my co-panellists, and felt quite protective, even motherly, towards them.

Lisa Oldfield continued to bemuse and confuse me. During the rehearsals and the first week of the show she would arrive looking distraught and complain bitterly about her father and husband. She claimed they previewed the tapes and told her she was dreadful, that she was hopeless, that she had no talent. I found it upsetting – the last thing any of us needed was to be undermined, especially by members of our own family. I felt desperately sorry for her. She was intelligent and yet vulnerable.

Yet with Lisa just when you were feeling your most sympathetic, the ground would suddenly shift. Early on in the show she made some on-air remarks about her childhood and came into the production office the next day, agitated. She needed, urgently, to change the biography she had written. She wanted to change the details of her life story because it was causing upset in the family. Yet another morning she came in with her mouth bruised and swollen and told us all she'd been kicked by a horse at the weekend. We believed it. By the time we were ready to go on camera she had totally changed her story (after being challenged by the canny hairdresser) – her lips had in fact reacted to 'injectables' given to make them appear fuller and more voluptuous. The contradictions went on and on.

Lisa also cried and vomited on camera. During a DIY segment she was asked to demonstrate a home fire extinguisher – the moment the fumes hit the air she started to throw up and had to dash from the studio. The same thing happened when we showed footage on camera of an eccentric English animal-rights campaigner eating corgi meatballs in Trafalgar Square to protest the royal family's fondness for fox-hunting.

On another occasion she started to cry and talked emotionally on camera about her miscarriages, totally taking the focus from the group discussion. And when we debated the issue of decriminalisation of certain illegal drugs she suddenly became hysterical, sobbing and saying that drugs had nearly ruined her life, that she had been drug addicted in her early twenties. Good grist for the gossip columns – the newspapers were full of it the next day.

Libbi and I were also concerned about how many of Lisa's political views were in fact her husband's. When our topics for the day had been decided she would sometimes phone him and take copious notes. Several times she hijacked a topic by going off on a completely different political tangent that none of us could really debate with her because she would suddenly be spouting facts and figures it would be impossible for us to refute on camera without time for some of our own research. I believe she was quietly taken aside and told to 'stick to the agreed topic'.

Working with Lisa was nerve-wracking. She had to be handled with great care. Yet in spite of all this there was something very engaging about her. She was quick-witted and funny, and appeared desperate to get on with us all. She just had an unpredictable side to her nature that was very hard to keep up with.

Zoe was a sunny, sweet-natured young woman who was impossible not to like. She had a dizzy blonde quality which could be infuriating at times, especially during on-camera discussions or interviews when she would make some offhand remark that could make her seem daffy. One question she asked, 'Will John Howard still be Prime Minister if Maxine McKew wins his seat?', became legendary in the media. Her lack of knowledge about current affairs was a tremendous disadvantage. It is impossible to debate issues with a person who is totally uninformed.

During our first week on air, the US vice-president, Dick Cheney, was in Sydney, staying with John Howard at Kirribilli House. In our morning production meeting I suggested we should discuss him and his Australian visit on the show.

'Who is Dick Cheney?' Zoe asked wide-eyed.

'Only the second most powerful person in the world,' I think I responded.

A few weeks later she asked a similar question when we mentioned the possibility of talking about Queensland's premier, Peter Beattie. She'd never heard of him. Often when we debated difficult or intense topics she'd break into an angelic smile and suggest we should all meditate more, or do yoga, or spend more time thinking lovely thoughts. She was not in the real world. She sometimes didn't appear to be listening to our conversations – it was as though she was sitting at the desk, waiting to slip in a funny line or a quip without really participating in what was supposed to be a reasonably intelligent debate. I liked her tremendously – she was, generous, funny and sweet – but she was on cloud-cuckoo-land.

Over the run of the show some hilarious incidents occurred. During the first few week, I didn't realise that the microphones attached to our clothes could be heard by absolutely everybody – even the executives on the third floor could tune in and listen to us if they chose to. It was not a good idea to make flippant asides, as I discovered the hard way. We were waiting to do the celebrity gossip segment where we crossed live to the *Woman's Day* office and chatted to poor Pete Timms.

I turned to Libbi and said, 'I hate this bloody segment.'

Immediately I heard Pete in my earpiece. 'Thanks, Mary,' he said.

Whoops.

There was also the Shelley Horton affair. Shelley had been one of the four women chosen for the earlier show that didn't get the go-ahead. She had been passed over for *The Catch-Up*. However Mia, Tara and Henrie really liked her and had decided to use her as a fill-in host if any of us wanted time off. Six weeks into the show Lisa wanted to take a few days' break, so Mia contacted Shelley and asked her to stand in. Shelley apparently sent an email to all her friends encouraging them to watch the show while she was on, 'even though I know you hate it'. One of her so-called friends leaked the email to the media and

Mia was furious. Shelley called us that weekend, crying and apologising profusely. She bought a huge bunch of flowers for all the hard workers in the production office. I felt sorry for her, but thought the whole incident was highly amusing, because it demonstrated to me so clearly that in the competitive world of show business, nobody has a true friend!

Another of our guest presenters had a problem with the bottle. Again I could smell it in the dressing room, and the second day she came on with us she appeared totally smashed. That said, she was hilariously funny and I don't think the audience would have been any the wiser.

I also had a bodice-ripping moment. Minutes before we were due on air the zip on the glamorous dress I was wearing broke (the dress was far too small). Our delightful assistant wardrobe manager, John, tried to repair it, tried to pin it, and then tried to get the dress over my head, but it was just too tight. The only way he could remove it so I could leap into the 'standby' outfit was to physically tear the dress from my body. I was literally running down the corridor to the studio; getting dressed as I went.

It really helped being able to see the funny side of the circumstances we found ourselves in and to laugh at the absurdity of the whole situation. We were all trapped by the lure of a success and even though the odds were probably always stacked against us, we were giving it our best shot and giggling a lot along the way.

15

After each show there was a debrief, and a planning session for the next day. Afterwards I would pick up my research materials and stagger back to my small apartment in Milsons Point to collapse in an exhausted heap. Before the show actually started, I had had visions of spending lots of time socialising with my Sydney-based friends and relatives and going to movies or live shows, but the job was just too draining and there was also a lot of reading and research to do every day for forthcoming episodes. In truth, living in a small apartment in the city was a rather lonely and depressing existence. I was inclined to fall into a chair and look at the previous day's episode to try to get a perspective about how the show was going (I often cringed at the clumsiness of some of the interviews). With no one to come home and talk to in the evenings, I drank too much wine in an attempt to unwind.

One night, however, Libbi asked me to her place for dinner, to meet her partner Stewart and their little boy. I was tired, but thought it was probably a good idea if we spent some downtime together. It was a lovely relaxing evening which revealed a side of Libbi I hadn't seen before. At work she was focused and driven, trying to pull the show together. Often she appeared embattled. At home with her family the softer side of Libbi was apparent, and it made me realise how great the burden of surviving in the world of television can be. At that point I decided that I really liked and respected Libbi and that, if nothing else, we could support each other through the difficult times ahead.

Amid all the pressure of putting the show together every day we limped along, week after week, with bad reviews and negative publicity, including personally targeted gossip which destabilised the team. I was always amazed when we turned up Monday morning and still had a show to do. Then the writing began to appear on the wall. The first hint was when the WIN Network that covers dozens of regional stations around the country dropped the show. It represented a huge percentage of our audience. We weren't advised that this was going to happen – the first we knew of it was when David, at home at the farm, turned the TV on to watch the show and discovered it was no longer running on our local station.

Next, Eddie McGuire stood down as CEO. He was our champion and, more importantly, Mia Freedman's biggest supporter – he had helped her to make the huge career leap from being an high flyer in the world of women's magazines to becoming a television executive, a leap that must have infuriated a lot of people who had worked in television for decades. She was a newcomer with a prominent media profile and a lot of power, and that didn't sit well with everyone. For the first few months Mia was with us all the way – she was at every early-morning production meeting and every pre-show production meeting, and always hanging around the control room, and then afterwards in our dressing room to encourage us or just debrief. Suddenly we stopped seeing her around. It was as though she had vanished somewhere on the third floor.

The final nail in the coffin, from my perspective, was the Logies. There was a lot of hype at the station about the annual TV awards ceremony. Our red carpet frocks were chosen with great fanfare –

indeed we were given three choices and the audience were asked to vote for their favourite. The awards would be held in Melbourne on a Sunday night. Zoe and I flew down on Friday afternoon after the show – a big mistake. We went partying with a bunch of her delightful, zany friends, and I ended up at six in the morning in a nightclub somewhere, wondering what on earth I was doing. A little too much excitement.

Lisa arrived in time for lunch with us on Saturday. I only lasted an hour in the restaurant, then staggered back to bed for the afternoon, realising that if I didn't pace myself I would be exhausted by the time the Logies came around the following night. That evening I found Lisa and Zoe wandering very much the worse for wear around the lobby of our hotel. I was worried that the place was swarming with photographers and managed to entice them up to one of our rooms to order some food, hoping it would settle things down. Lisa stopped off in her own room, then suddenly appeared wandering down the corridor wearing a very revealing nightdress. I could tell that we were heading for another wild night. I opted out early, hoping like mad they would be sensible and get some sleep.

Libbi arrived on the Sunday morning to total chaos. She went looking for Lisa and found her in a distressed state; it seemed that Lisa had been violently ill all over her hotel room. Nobody really knew where Zoe was. We had been asked to present ourselves for hair, make-up and wardrobe by 11.30 am. This was when I realised that our hotel was across the road from the main venue for all the action, Crown Casino, which was perhaps the most telling clue of all. We were expected to wander back and forth across the road to get prepared for our red-carpet walk at 5.30 pm. All the other on-camera personalities were staying in glamorous suites in the main hotel at Crown. At one point, mid-afternoon, Libbi and I found ourselves in a situation where we were obliged to cross the street past thousands of television fans who were lining up to watch the spectacle, wearing our old jeans and with our hair in rollers. It took a lot of the glitz and glamour away from the day and made it obvious to me that we were not really high priority Channel 9 personalities, just minor celebrities a long way down the totem pole.

Somehow Lisa and Zoe scrubbed up for the night. But while they were interviewing various celebrities on the red carpet, Libbi and I managed to get totally lost within the bowels of the hotel. At one point we elbowed our way through a throng of fans and ducked under the gold ropes, only to be coolly ejected from the event by a security guard.

I found the Logies ceremony boring in the extreme, and ducked out during one of the commercial breaks and simply went to bed. I didn't make it to the after party. Early next morning none of my co-presenters appeared in the hotel foyer when the taxis arrived to take us to the airport. We had to be back in Sydney by nine that morning to prepare for our show at midday. I made panicky phone calls to the production office and asked various people at the hotel to bang on doors to get the girls moving. At the airport I sat alone, despondently wondering what on earth I would do if they didn't show up. How could we do a show? Suddenly Lisa appeared in a Russian-style black fur coat and Cossack hat, looking for all the world like Cruella de Vil from *101 Dalmatians*, and wearing an expression like a stunned mullet. Then Libbi turned up, dressed in a flimsy sun frock and minus her shoes. With all the back and forth between hotels the day before, somehow most of her clothes and accessories had gone astray. She only had her glamorous Logies gown (red and strapless and not suitable for a 7 am flight) and this little dress.

Zoe didn't make the plane. She was eventually shaken awake by hotel security and caught a later plane that had her at Channel 9's Artarmon studios just in time for a dash of make-up. What a motley crew we looked. If the network's executives had been harbouring any doubts about dropping the axe on our show, I think that day's performance destroyed any compassion they may have felt for us.

16

When the axe fell, it fell quickly. Mia and Tara hadn't attended the Logie awards. They made excuses, but it was obvious to me that something was going on behind the scenes. Several weeks later in early June, while we were waiting to do our live cross to Pete Timms in the middle of a show, he suddenly spoke into our hidden earpieces.

'What's happened to Mia?' he asked.

Libbi and I exchanged glances. Before we could ask him what he meant, we realised all our microphones had been switched off by someone in the studio control room so that he could no longer hear us and we could not answer him.

'Something funny is going on,' Libbi whispered to me and then, suddenly, we were back on air.

At the end of the show we were asked to go directly to the production office. Mia was there, along with several network heavies. She announced her resignation to the assembled production staff, and we were then told by one of the executives that Friday's show would be our last. People were crying – it was a very emotional scene. All of us knew, from the production assistants to the studio director, that the ratings had been falling and the show was struggling to keep its head above water. But we had always been promised that we would be given until the end of the year, regardless of ratings, to get established and find a loyal audience. I knew this was the standard line taken by TV networks dealing with struggling new programs, but many of the others seemed to have taken these promises as gospel.

While the rest of the team appeared distraught, I felt a huge surge of relief. All the tension and pressure I had been carrying around for months slipped away. I realised that the show had completely consumed my life. I had been living and breathing the crazy, phoney world of daytime television for the last five months, but now I was finally free.

I felt desperately sorry for Mia and Tara, who had put their hearts and souls into this show. I was also devastated for our team of young producers, who had worked ridiculously long hours to keep the show bubbling along. Five hours of live television a week takes a tremendous amount of effort behind the scenes, and they had worked themselves half to death because of their commitment to us and to the program. Most of them would now be unemployed.

Sadly and unfairly, the media laid most of the blame for the show's failure squarely at Mia Freedman's feet. The newspaper columnist Sandra Lee wrote: *Freedman missed what the audience intrinsically knew: there was no chemistry no matter how much the women said they liked each other.*

I couldn't help but think that perhaps it was my fault because I hadn't believed in The Secret!

Lisa, whose name was also often mentioned during that week by television columnists writing about what went wrong, decided to take the blame publicly.

'My only regret is that I dragged down three brilliant performers,' she said. 'I know I'm crap. I'm sorry that I brought this upon them.'

Some saw it as a shameless strategy to get her photograph in the newspaper yet again, but I couldn't help but feel she genuinely blamed herself to some extent. She lacked confidence and took feedback from viewers and media very much to heart. During the run of the show she would dash back to the dressing room and immediately fire up her laptop computer, logging on to *The Catch-Up* website to read the blogs from irate viewers. She would read out loud the negative ones about herself and, despite her bravado, I could tell she was badly hurt by some of the more cutting remarks. You have to be very thick-skinned to cope with the deeply unpleasant comments made by some members of the audience. My way of dealing with the criticism was to avoid looking at the TV pages of newspapers and magazines, and I didn't read the website. I was happy to remain blissfully ignorant.

In many ways, the casting of Lisa had been a risky decision. Although her emotional sensitivity didn't surface immediately, she was more or less 'set up' as the conservative voice, and the fact that Libbi and I were often strongly opposed to her views meant that for the entire run of the show she must have felt pitted against us. It was a bit like leading a lamb to the slaughter!

In my view there were many, many factors stacked against the show's success. Mia was inexperienced in television and had to struggle against the internal politics within the Nine Network. It's almost impossible to make a program unless there's great support at the executive level. From a production perspective I don't think there was ever a clear view of how the show would work. It was like an evolving experiment from day one, with continual changes that must have confused our audience. Our time slot changed from 1 pm to midday, our seating positions on the panel changed, and we were asked to alter our debating styles. At first, we were directed to remain friendly at all times, but by the end the producers were devising a segment to be called The Bear Pit, which was intended as a free-for-all. They wanted more controversy and believed that if we had more heated debates we would attract media attention, as *The View* had done in the US. If the show had kept going I am sure it would have developed into a daily public slanging match with Libbi and me on one side, and Lisa on the other – so much for the original concept of 'agreeing to disagree'.

I have not kept in contact with Lisa. But several weeks after the show folded, I called her on her mobile phone and she told me she'd been very unwell. To me, the fact that she became ill so soon after the show was axed was telling. Like all of us, she must certainly have felt the strain.

I've seen Zoe a couple of times since the show and we phone or text each other just to keep in touch. She has continued doing voiceover work for television and radio commercials, but at the time of writing was still looking for another permanent job. Financially, it's been quite a struggle for her to keep going. Libbi and I established a strong friendship and went on to work together presenting a summer radio show for the ABC.

In spite of all of this, I wouldn't have missed *The Catch-Up* for the world, and after the show was canned I didn't feel any sense of failure. I was fortunate, I expect, in being the oldest cast member, because I wasn't as driven to succeed on television as the others. My career has always been primarily as a writer and I saw the show as a bit of a bonus – an opportunity to experience something totally different – and not as a major stepping stone. I also felt homesick for David and the farm during those long, tough weeks living in the city, living and breathing nothing but Channel 9. I wanted to spend more time with my daughter and my sister, both of whom were needing me. I had a cookbook to finish writing, a garden that was crying out for some attention and I was also hoping to get away to France at some stage soon.

Everyone involved in *The Catch-Up* had worked incredibly hard, and at times we really achieved what the program set out to do. As someone who relishes extreme experiences – and there's no question that living for nearly six months in the world of daily live television is about as extreme as it gets – I loved every minute. *Non, je ne regrette rien.*

17

As I grow older I appreciate that good health is more important than beauty or fame or wealth. I have been lucky to have been pretty healthy for most of my life, but when I do fall ill the results tend to be dramatic. There was the bout of viral meningitis I succumbed to when Miriam was just a baby. I was in my early twenties, and working full time, when I woke in the middle of the night with the most devastating headache. I don't normally get headaches, even after a wild night out. David called the doctor who immediately recognised the symptoms, and I was in intensive care within the hour and then flat on my back for two weeks until I was able to lift my head from the pillow.

Mysteriously, I had two further bouts many decades later. The first was in 2000, only months before I went to France on that first adventure, and there was another the following year. Both episodes were frightening, and the doctors, including a specialist immunologist, were perplexed at how a normal, healthy woman could experience three episodes of the same virus in a lifetime (although I believe there is a syndrome of recurrent viral meningitis which is now quite well documented).

David believes that because I am a high-energy person, always on the go, always having unrealistic expectations of myself, and always 'overachieving', I push myself and push myself and then fall in a heap. I am sure there is an element of truth in this theory. There is also the inescapable factor of ageing. From the age of fifty we are more susceptible to conditions such as arthritis, high blood pressure and type 2 diabetes. Exercise and a good diet help to keep problems at bay, but nevertheless more and more of us discover ailments that may have been lurking in the background for some time.

When *The Catch-Up* was laid to rest, David was in the UK working on projects after his annual trip to the Cannes Film Festival, and I had to fly back to the farm and get on with my life alone. The country around Bathurst was experiencing bitter mid-winter weather, but I didn't mind. I secretly relished the idea of some total peace and quiet. Indeed the prospect of solitude had never appeared so appealing before. I set myself up in the kitchen at the farm and started writing my family cookbook. It was early June and very cold, so I lit the wood cooker and moved my computer onto the breakfast table so that I could get down to writing in earnest. It was such fun, after the pressure of television, to delve into old photograph albums, lingering over the task of selecting pictures, and searching through my mother's cookbooks and collection of recipes to find old favourites. It was strange having to write the recipes down, as so many had been learned at my mother's side, and I had never bothered to measure ingredients or take a note of the cooking time. It had all been done by feel and instinct rather than science.

Writing was a form of therapy, comforting after the whirlwind of the first half of the year. I set myself a deadline of late July to finish the work, and booked myself a return ticket to France, where I planned to have a little downtime in August and September, as well as picking up the threads of a second book I had started writing but put to one side because of the television show.

Before I flew out, I was feeling a bit rundown and lacking in energy. I also noticed that my mouth was always dry, and suspected I was dehydrated.

I increased my water intake, jumped on the plane, and fled to my village house where I was welcomed by my usual contingent of friends, and immediately swung into a busy round of socialising – lunches and dinners and afternoons sitting around quaffing rosé and talking. The weather was hot, and I was walking a lot, so my feeling of dehydration continued. One night I woke in the early hours to discover that the inside of my mouth had adhered to my gums. I literally had no saliva in my mouth and no matter how much water I drank I still felt as though my mouth was, to use that delightful Australian phrase, like the bottom of a cocky's cage.

Next morning I opened my computer, checked my emails and then typed *dry mouth* into a search engine. There were hundreds of websites but the ones that leapt out at me were those on Sjögren's syndrome, an inflammatory disease of the autoimmune system that mostly affects women and usually presents in the forty-five to fifty-five age group. The causes are unknown, but there is evidence to suggest that viruses, including meningitis, can trigger it. Hah, I thought, it was all adding up. I quickly read website after website; the more I read, the more depressed I became.

The two main symptoms of Sjögren's were reportedly dry mouth and dry eyes. It dawned on me that my eyes had been feeling dry and gritty of late. It seems that the glands that provide moisture to the eyes and mouth become damaged by inflammation and cease working properly. The symptoms are uncomfortable and irritating, but are usually manageable with eye drops and mouth gels. Extra dental care is recommended, because without a constant flow of saliva, the teeth and gums are at greater risk of developing problems.

The medical websites went on to detail some of the rarer and more sinister complications of Sjögren's. Some patients developed systematic lupus erythematosus (attacking joints, kidneys and skin) and rheumatoid arthritis. Great. One site described it thus:

> *Sjögren's is the attack on moisture-producing glands by the body's own immune system, eventually destroying these glands. Sjögren's syndrome can also cause problems in other parts of the body, including the joints, lungs, muscles, kidneys, nerves, thyroid gland, liver, pancreas, stomach, and brain. What causes this malfunction is not yet known, however genetic, immunologic, hormonal, infectious factors are all suspected to be involved.*

They also reported that a percentage of Sjögren's sufferers went on to develop lymphoma, cancer of the lymphatic system. I suddenly realised I had another connection with this condition. Years before, when we were living in Leura, we had 'weekend neighbours' who became very good friends. Audrey and Barry had transformed their plain fibro cottage in a ramshackle garden into a small timber bungalow in typical Blue Mountain's style; the garden had also blossomed under Audrey's tender loving care.

We often chatted over the fence while pulling weeds or shovelling compost on a Saturday or Sunday, and always got together for a drink when our day's work was done. One afternoon, while I was having tea with Audrey, I noticed she was having trouble talking because her mouth was so dry. She used a spray, and explained to me that she had a syndrome that affected her saliva glands and tear ducts. It was irritating but not really much of a problem, she said. I didn't think too much of it.

In time, they sold their house and bought another property in the Mountains, and we no longer saw much of them. Out of the blue I had a call from Barry at their Sydney home. Audrey had just undergone surgery and chemotherapy for lymphatic cancer; she would love to see me if I was coming down. I visited a few weeks later, and found that although her spirit was still strong, she seemed very weak. I was shocked: my friend had always been such an active, energetic woman, slaving for hours non-stop in the garden. Audrey mentioned that the cancer was connected to Sjögren's syndrome. Sadly, after a period of remission, her cancer overwhelmed her, and she died within two years of the diagnosis. David and I were deeply saddened as we had loved Audrey, and we knew how devoted Barry was to her.

Siting alone in France in front of my computer, I felt anxious and fearful. I needed a medical opinion.

Madame Coppe is the popular local doctor in a nearby small rural town, and although her bedside manner is abrupt she is renowned for her knowledge and diagnostic skills. I went to see her, detailed my symptoms and neatly informed her of my self-diagnosis. She smiled knowingly and made a slightly disparaging remark about patients using the internet for medical advice. But after a brief examination, she confirmed my fears: I did indeed have Sjögren's. She did not appear overly alarmed, and simply wrote out a list of various medications, gels and eye drops that would help alleviate the symptoms. She also suggested that I consult my GP on return to Australia and have some tests to eliminate the possibility of further complications.

My initial reaction was one of shock, mingled with something like anger. I didn't want to have *any* illness, especially one with such uncomfortable symptoms and the possibility, down the track, of much more serious consequences. The idea of developing cancer certainly frightened me: four percent of people with Sjögren's develop lymphoma, a rate considerably higher than among the general population.

I phoned David and tried to describe what was going on without alarming him, which was difficult because any illness tends to make him very anxious. I also emailed the children to let them know, and told several of my friends in France. I decided that if my immune system was under assault the best thing I could do was to lead the healthiest lifestyle possible, which meant drastically cutting back on my consumption of wine. Needless to say, my drinking cronies were startled and somewhat regretful at this development. I kept returning to the internet for further information. The word 'incurable' seemed to leap off the screen, and while I knew my condition was by no means a death sentence, some of the implications were so serious I couldn't stop thinking about them.

But it's amazing how quickly we humans adjust to changed circumstances. After a few days I stopped researching Sjögren's because I recognised that every time I went on the internet it was just causing me worry. After a week I simply ceased dwelling on the diagnosis – except when when my eyes and mouth became extremely dry during the night. Soon I decided that there was no point dropping so many of the things I love about living in France – the food and wine in particular. There were a lot more important and pressing things going on within my family back in Australia, and it helped me to gain a more balanced perspective about my own situation.

Nevertheless, when I returned home in late August I made sure I consulted my local doctor and had a battery of tests to check the status of my immune system and my kidney function. The results were fine. There were no signs of any further progress of the disease – I was pronounced healthy.

The final upshot is that I have to take extra care of my teeth by having regular check-ups and cleaning. My eyes react badly to cold and wind, so I should wear protective goggles when I go out in the garden early in the morning. And I anticipate annual blood tests will help with early diagnosis of any further developments.

Plenty of worse things can happen in mid-life, but being diagnosed with Sjögren's made me think long and hard about the next few decades. Shall I be a healthy older woman, exercising and working hard in the garden and cooking up family feasts when the tribe descends? Or will I be sickly and frail and beset with medical complications that compromise my active lifestyle? My philosophy is that I should just continue living my life as I have always done – at full throttle. I could ease back, become a health fanatic, meditate, experiment with alternative therapies and join a support group. Yet there's no proof that it will make much difference in the end. If my disease progresses it will undoubtedly do so regardless of what efforts I make to control it. I prefer to think positively and have as much fun as I can in the knowledge that whatever happens, even if I get run over by a bus tomorrow, I've had a fantastic, full and happy life.

18

On the day that the blood from my mother's aortic artery started leaking into her chest cavity, she was stoic and silent. Our son Ethan, then sixteen, confronted her in the late afternoon and asked if she was feeling all right.

She responded, with some irritation, 'No I'm *not* all right. I think I'm dying. But don't tell your mother. She'll be upset.'

It's the story of my life. Well my adult life, anyway. My family protects me by skirting around plain truths that may upset me.

Am I so fragile, so vulnerable, that people close to me avoid telling me their problems? Are they so frightened of bursting my bubble and shattering my illusions that they think it's better to keep me in the dark?

I am an optimist, but being a positive person can have a downside. Always being cheerful, being up and happy and on top of things, can close the door to the possibility of acknowledging the darker, more difficult aspects of being alive.

I always imagined I was open and down to earth. That I invited conversation and discussion and debate from those around me. I believed, quite vehemently, that I encouraged my children to talk at the dinner table and to be quite frank and honest in expressing their views and their thoughts and their perceptions. I recall priding myself on the fact that our children never complained or demanded. They didn't whinge for the latest toy; they didn't come home from school in tears because of a playground squabble; they didn't moan (well, not very often) about their teachers or the injustice of their school system or the bully on the bus. They just got on with their lives.

Other people's children were quite different. I knew one couple who made an appointment to mediate with the parents of a child who had a lunchtime spat with their daughter. Both girls would have been nine at the time, and the dust-up had been over some trivial matter but had escalated into a full scale slanging match. On another occasion a mother phoned me to see if Miriam was OK after a heated row with her best friend (the woman's daughter). The other child was in shreds, inconsolable. Miriam was cheerfully playing in the backyard with her brothers. She hadn't made mention of the dispute at afternoon tea, and she didn't look even slightly ruffled. When I questioned her about the fight she just shrugged. 'It wasn't anything much,' she said. I wondered what all the fuss was about.

My children didn't tell me if they had been in trouble for forgetting their homework. I expect by the time they got home from school they had just forgotten. They didn't tell me about detentions (unless there was a note I had to sign) or about being kept in at lunchtime or being sent to the headmaster for some act of bad behaviour. I'm sure these things must have happened from time to time, but I never heard about them. By the same token they often forgot to give me school notes or to notify me about forthcoming excursions, and they always, *always* announced that they needed a special costume for some performance at the school assembly ten minutes before they were due to leave the house and catch the school bus.

It didn't occur to me that my children were particularly secretive or that they were protecting themselves from getting into trouble by not reporting various aspects of their lives outside the front gate. I just thought they were normal children, so caught up in their own world and so preoccupied and disorganised that these ripples in their daily lives were just that. Ripples.

So much of that period of their lives is vivid to me. Their glowing, healthy skin and thick, tangled hair. Morning hair-brushing was always a struggle. The kids' gangly arms and legs and skinny shoulderblades, poking out pathetically in spite of the fact that they devoured every meal as though it was their last. Their wobbly baby teeth replaced by oversized teeth always in need of a good scrub (another source of my nagging). It was certainly the most carefree period of my life, when the children were young and full of life and energy and very much, I believed, under my control and protection. I saw myself as a mother hen. Not a fierce and protective mother hen on the prowl for predators and ready to attack anyone glancing sideways at my clutch of chicks. More the warm and plump mother hen who spread her wings every night and invited the chicks to snuggle up, safe and warm.

No parent can know everything that happens in the life of their child. It isn't possible to be with them twenty-four hours a day, watching over and protecting them from possible dangers. But it is possible to be in tune with them. To read the signs and signals that tell you things are not quite right in their world. It is possible to keep an open line of communication, never broken, allowing them to tell you if things are troubling them. Or so I thought.

There was a local parish priest who ran an after-school gym for primary school children, and my children were very keen to join in with their friends. Two hours every Wednesday from 3.30 until 5.30 pm. A great break for the mums and a chance for the children to burn off some of their boundless energy.

Miriam and her three brothers went with a handful of their classmates and at the end I was waiting to pick them up. They tumbled into the car, full of noise and excitement – all except Miriam, who was unusually quiet. Later that evening, after dinner, I asked her how she'd enjoyed Kids' Club, as it was called.

'It was OK but I don't think I want to go again,' she said.

'Why not? Wasn't it fun?'

'I don't like that Father Tom,' she said. 'He squashed me on the mat.'

'Oh well, you don't have to go if you don't enjoy it.'

Now what could be a more descriptive danger signal to a parent than that? *He squashed me on the mat.* I knew that Miriam wasn't at all sporty – in fact her bad eyesight and glasses had made sport a bit of a nightmare which she chose to avoid at any cost. So I dismissed it as that. She didn't like all the gymnastics and tumbling and the roughness of the boys.

Eighteen months later Father Tom disappeared from the community, and soon afterwards was charged with molesting young girls. It would seem the Kids' Club was one of places where he most frequently committed these offences. He obviously hadn't got very far with Miriam, but that's not the point. I was her mother, her confidante, her protector. She had told me quite clearly that something unpleasant had occurred and I had, for whatever reason, chosen to ignore it.

It gets worse.

Click forward to August 2007, the time I spent in France, ostensibly working on a new book but also having a break after those five exhausting months on *The Catch-Up*. Like a bolt from nowhere came an email from Miriam that alarmed and upset me.

More than six months had passed since she and Rick split up and she appeared, to me, to be coping extremely well. Too well, in many ways. I knew she was having counselling, and I thought it was a good idea. I hoped both of them were having counselling – maybe even marriage counselling. The email she sent that day was, she said, part of her 'homework'.

It was angry. Reproachful. In brutal terms she told me that from the age of eleven until she turned fifteen she had been sexually abused by a teenage boy in our neighbourhood. Not every day. Sometimes not for months at a time. But random attacks of sexual violence that included biting and digital penetration.

She had hidden it from me. She didn't want to cause a problem for me or our family or for the family of the boy involved. She just put up with it and tried to avoid him as much as possible. She avoided being in situations where she was alone and developed strategies to protect herself as much as possible.

I was there all the time. I worked from home. I cooked dinner every night. I talked to my kids. I knew their teachers and went to endless P&C meetings. I worked in the school canteen and helped with fundraising. Encouraged sport and music and never missed a concert.

Why didn't I know this was happening under my very nose? Was I so caught up in the appearance of being a 'great mother' that I simply didn't connect with them on a deeper, more personal and, quite frankly, more important level? Didn't Miriam trust me enough to tell me? Did she think I wouldn't believe her? She apparently had bruises and bite marks and other visible signs of abuse. She could easily have shown me. I would have believed.

The story doesn't end there.

Some years later, when she was the mother of four boys herself, Miriam actually told me about these attacks. Not in graphic detail, although she made reference to having been 'jumped' by a boy at the bus stop after school. This wasn't very long ago – maybe five years; we were sharing a glass of wine and reminiscing about the 'good old days' when Miriam and her brothers were growing up. She talked about being an awkward, gangly teenager with braces and glasses and painfully thin legs. Then she told me that this particular boy had often pounced on her. I must have closed the conversation down or moved on to another topic. I can remember her telling me, but at the time nothing untoward about the situation registered in my mind.

Head in the sand. Head in the sand. No wonder she was angry with me. I wasn't there to acknowledge her pain when she was a child, when she was being attacked. And years later, when she told me, I just glossed over it. Was I incapable of admitting that bad things happen and they can very easily happen close to home? Was my rosy, naïve view of the world another symptom of my 'fantasy life'?

I phoned Miriam from France in the middle of the night. We both cried.

'Why didn't you tell me?'

'I did. I told you.'

'You did, I know you did. I remember the conversation now but it honestly didn't impinge. Why on earth didn't you tell me at the time it was all happening?'

'You didn't give me permission to, Mum. You never wanted to hear anything bad.'

I feared her observation was accurate. I didn't want my life to be touched by anything negative.

My phone conversation with Miriam left me in a sombre and reflective frame of mind.

All I had ever wanted was a big, happy family. I was wedded to the whole rose-covered cottage and picket-fence notion of family life. A vegetable patch, chickens scratching in the backyard, bread baking in a fuel stove, vegetable soup simmering on the hob and rosy-cheeked children running in from the garden for afternoon tea. Grandma knitting by the open fire and perhaps a basket of kittens purring nearby.

Well, that's what I created. Consciously, and with plenty of hard work and love and humour, I made this fantasy real. I believed in this lifestyle explicitly and implicitly. In a funny way, for an atheist like me, it was my religion. It defined who I was, and where I stood in life.

Now, alone in my house in Frayssinet, feeling unwell after my diagnosis, and desperately worried about my daughter, I wondered if I had been kidding myself. For some time, I realised, I had been living at odds with my dream. It started to unravel when I first ran away to France and experienced a tantalising moment of freedom from my perfect life. I was happy to come home to the warm bosom of my family but there was no doubt a certain restlessness had set in. I had itchy feet, and uprooted David from our home of twenty-five years to live further west on a small farm. I went back to France, fell in love with another man, and created havoc in my happy home. I thrashed around for several years, unable to decide what I really wanted from my life.

When I was forced into a corner and had to make a decision about our future together – whether I would remain married to David or leave and make my own way in the world – my love of family unity was by no means the only reason I decided to stay. I had taken a long hard look at my marriage and reached the conclusion that there was enough love left to repair the damage that had been done. But the happy family environment I had created around David and the children was an important part of my decision. I wasn't going to repeat the mistakes my parents had made. I believe we either unconsciously follow the patterns of our parents or deliberately set a different course. In David I had chosen a partner who was very different from my father – sober, faithful and careful with money. I had tried to avoid being like my mother in most ways, avoiding the constant arguments that punctuated her relationship with my father. I was a peacemaker rather than a battler. The atmosphere in my childhood home was unwelcoming to visitors and I rarely had friends over to play or socialise. I had been determined to make a home where the children would feel comfortable inviting their friends to stay, and especially during their teenage years the house at Leura had become a refuge for a floating population of youngsters.

Yet I was well aware that there were certain facets of my parents' personalities that were hard-wired into my character, despite my best efforts to avoid them. Just as blood is thicker than water, genes can triumph over even the best intentions.

19

The 1950s was a period of social repression. In the decades between the war and the sexual revolution of the 1960s, family life was portrayed as neat, clean and harmonious. A woman's place was in the home, and her role as a mother and homemaker had saintly overtones. It's easy to look back and laugh at the innocence of those days, but there was a dark side as well. Women were clearly subservient to their husbands, economically and in every other sense. I can remember in vivid detail how difficult life was for my mother when I was a child, and how she grasped the nettle to change her lot. She was ahead of her time.

Every week, my father handed my mother 'housekeeping' money that was intended to provide food for the table, buy clothing for the family, and pay a few small bills. After the rent he kept the rest of his not inconsiderable pay packet entirely for himself. It was his responsibility to pay the more substantial bills, such as telephone, gas and electricity. Sometimes he did, but if he lost at the races on a Saturday afternoon the accounts were shoved into a drawer and forgotten until the debt collector or bailiff banged on the front door early Sunday morning.

By the time I was seven my mother decided the family unit could no longer survive unless she got a job. In many ways, working probably saved Muriel. She had some cash flow and could pay the bills. She bought a car to get out and about in, and work provided an escape from her embattled domestic life.

She didn't manage money well, nor did she enjoy housework. Both she and my father smoked and drank heavily, which meant that although there was always plenty of food – and good food at that – there were rarely any new clothes for her or for us children. My father, on the other hand, spent lavishly on his wardrobe. He was a vain man and a dapper dresser. He could easily justify this expenditure because of the nature of his job as a newspaper editor, but in truth his appearance was important to him because he also enjoyed the company of women. It was hard for Mum to address his selfishness with him because he had a fiery, irrational temper and was violent when cornered in an argument. Feisty Muriel was not cowed by his outbursts, but I certainly was. And I have remained nervous of confrontation all my life.

These days, few women would tolerate a situation like my mother's. But in the 1950s, divorce was rare and carried a social stigma. I cannot remember any of my friends in primary school having divorced parents, but by the time I reached high school one or two were being raised by a mother alone. Divorce was mentioned in hushed terms. The women and children involved were pitied and, to some extent, scorned.

A neighbour of ours had four children; one day her husband simply disappeared. At first she spread the story that he was working interstate, but when he failed to rematerialise, even at Christmas, she took to her bed and the family situation became grim. No shopping was done, no cooking, no housework, and the children ran wild. The women in my mother's circle of friends discussed her situation but nobody tried to intervene or to offer assistance. They were either too polite or too inhibited to confront her with the reality that she had been deserted and needed help to raise her family. Eventually a relative came to the rescue and life for this family improved. Even years afterwards the fact of this woman's separation and possible divorce was never publicly mentioned. It seems almost unbelievable today.

There are now more avenues of escape – supporting mothers' benefits and women's shelters – that didn't exist then. Our society is much more understanding of women in this difficult situation – if perhaps still not as supportive as some would like. The courts generally favour women financially and in child custody, and although this is not always entirely fair, at least it means that women are no longer trapped in desperate or controlling marriages. There is a way out. For my mother there didn't seem to be any escape. She was emotionally tied to my father in spite of his awful behaviour and was frightened of being seen as a failure, by her own family in particular.

Once again, there it is: that terrible fear of failure. Just one of the things I've inherited from her.

My parents' love of alcohol and tobacco was more than just a reflection of the social mores of the time. My father had long bouts of depression and undoubtedly suffered from bipolar disorder, or manic depression as it was called then. He was born in 1910 and died in 1972, and the condition, although medically recognised, was not commonly diagnosed during his lifetime. Bipolar usually manifests in young adulthood with uncontrollable mood swings and soaring and plummeting energy levels that can often end in suicide. Untreated it can be a crippling disease that shatters the lives of sufferers and those who love them.

My father, I now believe, managed his symptoms by self-medicating with alcohol from a very early age. When I was younger, I assumed his obsessive drinking was a result of his job. It was almost mandatory for journalists to drink to excess – it went with the occupational territory. Hilarious anecdotes about the antics of drunken journos, here at home in Australia, or in London's Fleet Street or in New York, were legion in the mid-twentieth century. These characters, mostly male, seemed like romantic figures. Intelligent, risk-taking, charming and witty. They liked women and they enjoyed the adventure and the kudos of their work. The association of alcohol with this glamorous lifestyle was a heady and appealing mix. It obviously appealed to my mother who, as a beautiful young woman, leapt into this orbit and joined my father in a wild drinking spree in America where he was posted as a newspaper correspondent during World War II. So many of the photographs of them during that period testify to their hard drinking – puffy faces and bleary eyes. My mother told stories of reckless weekend parties and socialising. I'm amazed their livers made it back to Australia intact.

It always surprised me that my mother fell in love with a boozy, unreliable journalist because her own father, Augustus James Angel, was exactly that himself, and you would hope she might have learned to avoid the type. I'm not sure that Augustus rose much above the level of a court reporter, but he certainly enjoyed a drink or two and was unemployed (or unemployable) for long periods, much to the shame of his gentle wife, Ellen.

I was named Mary Ellen after my two grandmothers, who couldn't have been more dissimilar. My father's mother, Mary, was a hard-working, eccentric woman who ran a successful pawnshop business in Melbourne, and kept the family going financially in spite of her husband's failings. My father's father was a bit of a shady character. Mum told stories about him which she must have heard secondhand from Dad. He wasn't a very lovable man – certainly not nice to Mary and their five children – and he died at the age of fifty-three of cardiac failure and tertiary syphilis. I wonder how many generations back this legacy goes?

I don't believe I ever met our paternal grandmother in person, but in the days when she could remember such details from her childhood, my sister Margaret told me amazing stories about her. Mary didn't sleep on a conventional bed, but on a pile of newspapers and old clothes in the corner of a room above her shop. There was no bathroom and no toilet. Like other tenants of the slum area where they lived, she squatted over a hole in the ground in the courtyard out the back. During the war, when the city was teeming with drunken and sex-starved servicemen on leave, she carried a couple of pistols strapped to her waist. She was a force to be reckoned with, that earlier Mary Moody!

My mother's mother was quite the opposite: gentle and sweet and non-confrontational. She was, however, quite stubborn and proud and possibly, I believe, a bit of a snob. She cared very much what her neighbours in Haberfield thought and was deeply embarrassed by their poverty, going to great lengths to hide the fact that they often survived on food vouchers and other handouts. Mum was a cultured young woman for someone from a lower middle-class western suburb of Sydney in the 1930s. The fact that she studied ballet to quite a high level was amazing, given the family's fragile financial status. She went to symphony concerts and balls in elegant frocks that Ellen, a tailor, fashioned out of old curtains. In our black and white photographs she looks a million dollars, but I know that she gave most of her weekly wages as a secretary and later a trainee journalist to her mother. I suspect my attractive father was an escape from this depressing situation.

Attractive he was. A slender, handsome widower with two unhappy children who needed mothering. A fairly irresistible cocktail for a warm and sensitive young woman. I'm not sure if Mum already enjoyed a tipple when she met Dad or if she gave in and joined him in his daily libations. By the time they returned to Australia after the war she was, by all accounts, a seasoned drinker.

There is a difference between a drinker and a drunk, between a person who is fond of a social drink and an alcoholic. Much depends on the drinker's ability to continue functioning. If someone can drink every day and still hold their life together – still hold down a job and pay the rent – then they can't be an alcoholic, can they? I suspect that's what my father thought as he dodged and weaved his way through life with a glass in his hand and a flagon under his arm. He was a highly successful professional. Mum constantly reminded us of his elevated status, his high income, the respect that was afforded him in many circles. Then why did we have no money? And why didn't we own a house or car? Why did my parents run out of cash before week's end and need to pawn various household items to buy food and grog? Simple. My father was an alcoholic and it impacted on his life, the lives of his children, his marriage and, ultimately, his health.

I am not sure how much Dad drank as a younger man, but I expect it increased as his income did. I know that when I was a child he always had a 'heart-starter' around 8.30 am – a couple of shots of whisky on the way to work. He topped that up with beers during the day – a couple mid-morning, a couple at lunchtime, a couple mid-afternoon and a few more on the way home from work. Then he switched to claret, which he drank from a sturdy tumbler from the time he came home until he fell into bed quite early. He never looked very drunk to me – I was used to his florid face and quick temper – but he did look terribly hungover on a couple of occasions, usually after family get-togethers. His reputation at such gatherings was much talked about. I don't understand why he felt it was okay to get uproariously drunk and make a scene at these social events. I was told in hushed tones, decades later, of the night he gave my mother a black eye at her niece's twenty-first birthday. He wasn't welcome at family parties after that. Then, at my cousin's wedding, he managed to get drunk before the ceremony and bop some hapless friend of the family on the nose. Disgraced, he was sent home in a taxi – at vast expense – and next morning discovered he had managed to lose his glasses and his false teeth in transit. In social situations involving his work he was generally better behaved, but I have heard rumours of him throwing a fellow journalist down the steps of the Journalists' Club late one night. The story goes that the man was a dwarf, so I can't even begin to imagine what was going on there!

Mum drank too, but quite differently. She never imbibed during the day, except at the weekend. On Saturday mornings she and Dad would have a beer at the pub in Mosman after doing the shopping. On Sunday morning she would enjoy tumblers of sweet sherry while doing the ironing. Dad would be cooking the Sunday lunch and our small flat would be filled with the delicious aroma of the roasting food and the strains of Beethoven or Brahms could be heard from the stereogram. The atmosphere would be quite cosy – unless they decided to have a brawl after lunch, which was not that unusual. My brother, Dan, and I would retreat to the beach.

I grew up thinking that drinking was just a normal part of everyday life. Somehow I didn't associate it with the fact that we were always broke and that our parents fought constantly and made each other's lives miserable. I associated drinking with coping, with feeling better. If something went wrong, you had a drink. If you felt sad or depressed or worried, you had a drink. If someone made you angry or caused you frustration, you handled the situation by having a drink. In most households when there is a crisis someone makes a nice cup of tea. In our house, a bottle was opened.

Mum used to drink until she got drunk. Sometimes falling-down drunk or walking-into-the-wall drunk. Instead of being mortified, we treated Mum's drinking as a family joke. She was such a fantastically bright and engaging person that her weakness for alcohol wasn't just tolerated, it was celebrated. Instead of worrying about her daily consumption (although I did worry, terribly, in the last decade of her life) we gave her tacit approval by either ignoring it or applauding her outrageous behaviour. Her drinking meant that her beauty faded and she had a raddled, unkempt appearance that was in keeping with her lifestyle.

Because of her self-imposed rule against drinking before 5 pm, by five minutes beforehand she would be pacing around, looking at the clock and staring at the freezer where the ice cubes were in waiting.

On the dot of five o'clock she would fill a glass with ice and attack a bottle of Scotch whisky with great gusto. She did break from this discipline in times of trouble. There was a famous afternoon when our village in the Blue Mountains was thick with smoke, as bushfires raged in the valleys on both sides of the escarpment. We nervously attended to the recommended precautions, clearing around the house, filling the gutters with water, filling buckets and setting hoses in event of fire coming close to the house. Satisfied, Mum went next door and drank a bottle of whisky with our neighbour Mrs Batty, who wasn't a hardened drinker. Mum passed out on her sofa and the two of them eventually staggered back to our house in a pretty wretched condition (I am sure Mum drank more than her half of the bottle). Heaven knows how I would have coped had the fires really created a danger, evacuating four children, various cats, dogs, chickens and a paralytic mother!

Mum was slender and agile, and into her seventies could still hold a difficult ballet pose that required great flexibility. At times the children cringed at the sight of their grandma performing ballet movements in the living room in front of their friends, steadying herself with one hand on the back of the sofa, a glass of whisky in the other.

There was no point in stopping her drinking. She lived in a safe environment, was not in any physical or financial danger, and was surrounded by loving and supportive family members. I suppose if she had developed cirrhosis of the liver it would have been essential for her to stop, but although she was frail towards the end, she ate well and was still as sharp as a tack. In the end, it was the cigarettes that ultimately caused her death.

20

My first encounter with death in the family was the loss of my baby sister when I was two and a half years old. At that tender age I had absolutely no concept of death and, indeed, no real memory of Jane, who was ill in hospital for seven months before she died a few weeks short of her first birthday. However, the months leading up to her death were immensely fraught for the family, and for my mother in particular, because we had no car and the children's hospital at Camperdown was quite a hike from our place on public transport. The nursing staff didn't approve of lengthy visits from parents, especially from mothers, and towards the end I think Mum only made the heartbreaking journey to Jane's bedside about once a week, if that.

It was my family's response to the death that had a profound impact on my brother, Dan, and me. We were immediately bundled up by one of our sympathetic neighbours and taken to a farm near Goulburn, where we were lovingly cared for by her unmarried sister, who must have only been in her early forties, but seemed to my child's eyes to be positively ancient. It was weeks – probably more than a month – before Mum made the journey to collect us, I think by train, so I imagine that in spite of the warmth of our carers we were probably very confused, frightened young children.

Jane's name was not mentioned again for years and years – it was almost as though all traces of her had vanished. There was a funeral but I don't believe even my parents attended. To this day I am not sure whether my sister was buried or cremated or if, apart from a birth and death certificate, there is a record anywhere of her existence. One photograph of her as a gaunt, wide-eyed baby staring at the camera from her hospital bed is the only haunting evidence my mother had of her short life. So for me the emotions of fear and loss associated with death were felt from a very early age.

My father's death, many years later, was very different. He committed suicide, which was both shocking and disturbing, but also, strangely, a relief to me because of the turbulent time he and Mum had been through in the years leading up to it. They were in the process of a long and acrimonious marriage break-up, and he had slid further and further into alcoholism and depression, as had my mother. His demise seemed like a logical escape from the corner into which he had painted himself – not that there is anything strictly logical about suicide.

I was pregnant with Miriam at the time and the whole business of his death and the funeral and the aftermath seems like a hazy dream to me now. I know that I didn't grieve for him at the time – I didn't want sadness to impinge on the joy I was experiencing being with David and waiting for the birth of our first child. So I swept my father's death under the carpet and instead concentrated on helping my mother to climb out of her despair and hopelessness.

It seems amazing to me now that I was so blissfully unaware at that stage of my life, when I was pregnant with my first child, that any of those negative family characteristics could possibly be revisited on my own children. As far as I was concerned I was about to break the cycle, and to produce a new and healthy generation that would be free from the family demons. I was incredibly naïve.

When a newborn is shown off to the wider family by their proud parents, it's amusing to listen to relatives laying claim to individual features. His grandfather's chin, her Aunty Mary's nose, his sister's eyes. There's something to be said for this old custom. Children are an extraordinary amalgamation of everyone who has come before them, as family photos testify. One of our grandsons, Sam, looks astonishingly like photographs of David at the same age. My grand-daughter Ella resembles my daughter – her Aunt Miriam – but then again she also looks a lot like her own mother, Lorna.

I have a theory that the ultimate clue to what a baby will look like as an adult is evident at the time of birth. That first precious hour. Miriam didn't look like anyone we could identify when she was born – she just looked like herself – and as an adult she has mannerisms and speech patterns like me, but doesn't really resemble either of her parents. When they handed me Aaron, tightly swaddled with his small rumpled face on view, he looked so much like my late father that I could barely believe my eyes. As he grew from babyhood into a toddler, from a toddler to a schoolboy and into his teens, he looked nothing like my dad. Now, in his thirties, he once again looks so much like my father it's quite scary. Blond curly hair, a smooth complexion and intense blue eyes. Even his own children, when shown old photographs of their great-grandfather Theo, will ask, 'Is that my dad?'

So it would seem to me that the essence of the person is present from the moment of conception, not just the physical representation but also the way in which the mind works. Not just the outside, but the inside as well. I also strongly resemble my father. The same naturally frizzy hair, the same fair skin, the same driven, addictive personality and the same irreverent sense of humour. We both had careers as journalists and both maintained strong opinions on a wide range of subjects, politics in particular. Yet to me my father represented the epitome of all that was selfish and irresponsible. I have spent most of my adult life trying *not* to be like him, and sometimes I am not too sure I am winning the battle.

In some ways, my fears are the irrational product of a child's inability to distinguish herself from her parents. I am *not* my father, just as my son Aaron is *not* my father. But looking back on our family history now, from the vantage point of my late fifties, I can see realistically that I am the product of this history, no matter how much I have tried to avoid it. It's obvious that when you are a direct descendant of alcoholic and depressive parents and grandparents on both the maternal and paternal sides of your family, there is a pretty strong chance that you will carry one or both of the genes.

Maybe my half-brother, Jon, and my half-sister, Margaret, inherited their mother's genes, because neither of them have alcohol problems. My brother, Dan, and I both do. We all grew up in the same environment, experienced the same stresses and witnessed the same unhappiness, but Jon and Margaret never felt compelled to drink to excess. When Jon comes down for our family Christmas gatherings he has a few beers and an afternoon nap. In his own environment he only drinks when he goes out socially, perhaps to a community meeting, and he rarely plonks down in front of the TV with a cold can of beer unless he has visitors or there's a heatwave. He just isn't a drinker. Margaret used to enjoy a glass of wine with a meal but to my knowledge she was never a wild party girl. It's curious.

The problem with drinking is that it's insidious. It creeps up on you and dependence is just another glass of wine away. These days my brother, Dan, has his drinking well under control. Like our father he has suffered from depressive illness all his life. For many years he, too, controlled his mood swings by medicating himself with alcohol. A brilliant man – first a journalist then a scholar and university lecturer – his demons eventually caught up with him. He suffered a series of ruined relationships, mental breakdowns and periods of homelessness. Today, he has pulled his life together and although he lives alone he is a valued and highly regarded member of his community. He has a few drinks maybe once a week at his local, but he's basically a very fit and disciplined individual who has finally managed to wrestle the family disease under control. Given his journey, it's amazing he's still alive.

I love to drink. I love the effect of alcohol. The taste, the smell, the ritual, the associations of pleasure. David, on the other hand, is not a drinker. He loves a glass of good wine but when I am not at home he never opens a bottle to drink alone. He may have the odd gin and tonic, and certainly enjoys drinking wine when invited to dinner with our neighbours near the farm. But I suspect that if he never had another drink in his life, he wouldn't give a damn.

When we first met I only drank beer, in those days the journo's standard choice. I frequently bought a six-pack after work, and David was horrified by the rate at which I could consume can after can without batting an eyelid. One day he suggested we forgo the beer after work. I was furious. He said he thought I 'had a problem' and that, I must say, made me even more mad. Just to prove to him I didn't have a problem I stopped drinking. For a time.

During my pregnancies I drank very little, but I certainly remember the pleasure of that first tall glass of cool dark Guinness stout that I gulped down to kick-start lactation. Not a bad excuse. We were quite poor when the children were young, and I was a busy working mother, so drinking to excess was out of the question. For many years I brewed my own beer and drank a bottle every night while I was cooking. It was my 'reward' at the end of a hectic day of juggling work and family.

These days, especially in France, wine is affordable and I can stock the cellar with as much as I like. Wine goes with food and I love to cook, so it has become an entrenched part of my daily routine. Indeed, I find it hard to eat a delicious meal without a glass (or more) of wine, and am horrified to see other diners in restaurants quaffing fizzy drinks with a carefully prepared main course. If I were the chef I would ask them, politely, to leave immediately. On cold days at Yetholme I often cook 'a little hot lunch' for David and me to break the day. With wine? Of course.

David points out that the medically recommended quota of drinks for a woman is one per day, with at least two alcohol-free days a week. I can't imagine being able to stick to such a regime, but I worry that ultimately my drinking habits will impact on my life. I have regular blood tests, and to date my liver function has been fine – as was my mother's, even when she was drinking more than half a bottle of whisky a day. I suspect her resilience has lulled me into a false sense of security.

I tell myself that it would be easy to stick to a limit of a couple of glasses, but it doesn't ever seem to work out that way. When I have one I continue to keep pouring while I cook the dinner, chat to David and watch the evening news. I should stop drinking after the meal but I rarely do. I sip wine while checking my evening emails or catching up with the family on the phone. The only thing that stops me is bedtime. Mum used to watch television sitting up her in bed with a glass of Scotch. I haven't come to that. Not yet, anyway.

But I know I have memory lapses after drinking to excess, and it's more than possible that my failure to take on board Miriam's revelations about being molested as a child could easily be because we were both 'relaxing' over a glass of wine at the time. To date, my imbibing hasn't affected my ability to work. Indeed my schedule is extremely demanding and I rationalise that having a few drinks in the evening – or even at lunchtime – is a great way to relax and de-stress. The reverse is probably the truth of the matter, as alcohol is a known depressant.

David believes that my affairs were very much the result of socialising with too much alcohol. There's more than an element of truth to it, that being in a heady environment so far from home, spending hours over lunches and dinners with attractive, entertaining men, was a fatal combination. That the vast quantities of wine consumed greatly affected my judgement and decision-making. But I also believe there were many issues working away in the background of our relationship, and there was also my general mid-life feeling of restlessness.

From my perspective, looking back over the last thirty years, there's a more serious probability to confront. I can't help but wonder if alcohol played a larger role in my own family dynamics than I have ever wanted to acknowledge. I considered myself to be a social drinker but the reality was that I drank every evening. For many years I drank beer, but eventually it became wine – often cask wine, which makes it difficult to keep track of just how many glasses are being consumed over a number of hours. It's possible that my failure to see the problems my children were experiencing could easily have been because I was seeing the world through a haze.

When my mother was still alive, I certainly didn't drink to the same extent as her, but I joined her every evening in a glass or two before dinner, and I fear I was in denial about my increasing dependence on alcohol for a sense of wellbeing. The fact that I was functioning quite effectively in my work and that my home life appeared, to all intents and purposes, to be running along smoothly most of the time, gave me a false sense of security. My friends marvelled at my ability to accomplish so much, juggling my family and quite a high-powered career, but looking back I can see that I coped with the stress of 'keeping up appearances' by getting mildly sloshed every evening.

I am confronting this issue now because so much has happened over the past two or three years that I have been forced to stop in my tracks and take stock. I'm not necessarily blaming myself for problems my children may be experiencing as adults, nor am I wallowing in guilt, but I can see now that my laidback parenting style and my belief that 'every day should be a party' may well have impacted on their lives. I could continue with my head buried in the sand or I can be open and discuss my thoughts and fears with my family. I have chosen the latter way.

This begs the question: what to do? Alcoholism is a serious problem in Australia and can be linked not just to illness, but to crime and family breakdown. It's not something to be flippant or dismissive about. Yet in truth I can't see myself as a teetotaller. When I'm trekking I can go for days or weeks without a drink and it doesn't worry me in the slightest, but I simply can't imagine sitting at a table in France, eating fabulous food and sipping a glass of sparkling mineral water. Owning up to the fact that my drinking has sometimes had unhappy consequences is a good first step, and perhaps it will suffice. Time will tell.

21

I hadn't done a lot of writing during my trip to France in 2007 so I came home to the farm feeling a bit guilty that I had taken the time out at all. Even though he said very little, David was quietly seething. I had planned and booked the trip without consulting him first: I presented him with a fait accompli, and then jumped on the plane.

It's not unusual for me to avoid talking certain issues through with David, partly due to my avoidance of confrontation. I knew that if I had told him I wanted to go to France he would have put up objections and that would have resulted in an argument. So instead I booked a flight, then told him afterwards of my plans. My view is that as long as we own the house I want to keep going back. His view, as ever, is that we should sell. This is one reason why I conduct walking tours of south-west France every year, to help cover the costs of the place and reduce the financial strain, even if the other stresses of owning it must continue.

My first priority when I arrived home this time was to catch up with the family, so I drove over to Mudgee to celebrate Ella's seventh birthday. Aaron and Lorna had come a long way since the tense period of their initial separation, and things had really settled down, especially from the children's perspective. In some ways I have also adjusted to the change, although there have been financial and emotional ramifications that have worried me deeply. Anyone who thinks that separation and divorce are the easy way out is kidding themselves.

After the trip to Mudgee, I had to get organised for a four-day photo shoot at the farm. The cookbook I was writing had an entire section devoted to living and cooking at the farm, and both the publisher and designer wanted to feature the place in the book. We threw the doors open to a stylist, a photographer and a home economist; the plan was to cook and photograph at least thirty-five of the featured recipes over a period of four days. They also asked if we could gather as many of the family members around as possible, so they could be captured at a typical, full-on family lunch. Miriam flew from Adelaide with the four boys especially for the occasion. It was an enormous undertaking, but a great deal of fun.

The home economist made lists and shopped for all the recipe ingredients. The entire length of the farmhouse's central hallway was soon filled with neat stacks of food, sorted into piles according to the recipe and in order of preparation. Our daughter-in-law Simone, who was doing a part-time chef's course at TAFE, wanted to be part of the action, and her contribution proved invaluable.

I have a variety of cooking options in our kitchen at Yetholme. There's an old wood stove that has both an oven and cast-iron cooktop; there's a gas cooktop that also has a wok burner; and there's a large, modern electric stove. All of these appliances were going at full burn throughout the shoot. We cut and sliced and diced and mixed and made everything from banana custard to David's favourite recipe for san choy bao.

The four boys, all hollow legs, had been told to keep out of the way. They hovered on the back verandah like hungry magpies, taking in all the wonderful aromas from our test kitchen. As each recipe was completed it was 'arranged' by the stylist and then photographed under natural light. When each shot was completed I carried the cooling food back to the kitchen, where it was promptly devoured by my eager grandsons. It was hilarious. They hoovered down broad bean salad, a vast tiramisu, a roast leg of lamb with all the trimmings, roast pork and crackling, scones, roast chicken with stuffing, melon and ham, salad Niçoise and a platter of rich French cheeses, all in the course of one afternoon. They had no concern for the order of service; desserts coming before main courses wasn't a problem for them, only that the food kept rolling off the production line.

The family lunch was a triumph, with all of our grandchildren jammed around our long dining table – except for Isabella who, sadly, was having a bad episode of stomach problems, and was in Katoomba Hospital on a rehydrating drip.

Work such as this, where the whole family gets involved, is always enjoyable. Even though I had explained to the children what it was all about, they didn't really understand it fully until the book was published and they giggled to see themselves as part of it – lighting the dining-room fire, setting the table and climbing the big old cypress tree in the front garden. I am constantly amused and reassured by my grandchildren's blasé attitude towards my work. During the time I was trapped in Sydney, doing *The Catch-Up*, I had regular phone conversations with my Adelaide grandchildren because it was impossible to visit them while I was working such a gruelling schedule.

Chatting to the oldest, Eamonn, I asked how things were going at school and what sport he was playing, then casually asked if he had seen my TV show.

'What show?' he asked.

'Hasn't Mummy told you I'm doing a daily television show?'

'No,' was his uninterested response. End of topic.

Miriam later insisted that she told the kids about the show, but of course they would have been at school every day when it went to air, with no chance of ever seeing it. To me it was a very healthy sign that he didn't give two hoots if his grandmother appeared on daytime TV. He was much more interested in knowing when I was next coming down to Adelaide to take them all out for a slap-up yum cha lunch. Any delusions I might have had about being famous were instantly, and quite charmingly, squashed.

22

Alzheimer's is a condition that people joke about. It's such an obvious target for humour, involving older, powerless people who are confused and vulnerable and can't fight back, but there's probably also an element of fear in the jokes. For it's a disease that results in total helplessness, as tangled fibres in the brain gradually strangle every last shred of memory, killing brain cells, and eventually shutting the whole body down. It's horrific, in every possible way.

Sometimes it seems to me that having found my sister, Margaret, after forty-nine years of separation, I lost her again within a moment. As a result of her Alzheimer's she has forgotten everything. Everything. She was born in August 1933, twenty months after her brother, Jon. Their mother, Veronica, took her own life when Margaret was six years old – nobody really knows why.

Jon and Margaret's lives were certainly brighter when Muriel entered the scene as their stepmother, but by the time the family returned home to Sydney from Dad's American posting, they were under a lot of stress. Muriel was caring for two teenagers as well as two children under the age of three. They lived in a small, upstairs flat with a glassed-in verandah which served as a bedroom for Margaret, and me and my brother Dan (fourteen months younger than me) when we arrived on the scene. A teenage girl and two babies in one small room. The family had no car and no labour-saving devices; there was a dark, dingy laundry in the basement equipped only with a gas copper and wringer. Mum was soon exhausted from having two babies in rapid succession, and she lost interest in housework and keeping in touch with her friends and family. Dad was drinking heavily and she was drinking quite a bit too, in spite of her successive pregnancies. It was a recipe for domestic disaster.

Dan was an acute asthmatic in the days before drugs had been developed to control breathing difficulties. He was also highly intelligent and highly strung. I remember lying in bed at night listening to him rhythmically banging his head against his pillow and moaning until finally, exhausted, he fell asleep. I can't imagine why Mum didn't come to comfort him – I recall her telling me in detail about the nights she sat up with him when he was in the throes of a severe asthma attack, and I'm sure she did. However I believe his almost nightly need for attention was ignored and I have been told that his 'head banging' could have been a sign of emotional neglect.

I was a healthy and cheerful baby, but from a very young age I was certainly frightened by our father's frequent explosions of anger, and often lay in bed listening to my parents' protracted and heated rows in the next room. Margaret must have been even more acutely aware of the situation. She was called on to help my mother with 'the children', and I believe that before and after school she was my primary carer while I was a baby and toddler. Then she left. On her eighteenth birthday she simply packed her bag and left the family forever, never looking back. Doing her best, I am quite sure, to forget.

At first, Margaret lived with the family of a student friend from East Sydney Tech, where she had recently started a three-year course to qualify as an art teacher. She found a part-time factory job and supported herself until she graduated, then she taught art in various country schools until leaving for the UK. She went on to Canada where she continued to work as a teacher while furthering her qualifications, completing not one but two master's degrees, and eventually being awarded a PhD in art education.

She made no attempt to contact the family, no doubt fearing that if she called our father might answer the phone. She knew how angry he was at her leaving, because there had been a terrible family row on the day of her departure. So she effectively closed the door on further communication.

In most circumstances a person who had reached Margaret's level of Alzheimer's would have been placed in a care home of some description. They would have been given a lot more anti-anxiety and sedating drugs to make them more passive and manageable. However, Margaret's husband, Ken, is devoted to her care and does all he can to ensure she remains at home for as long as is possible.

Once I had accepted Margaret's condition and the distressing downhill spiral of the disease, I determined that I should spend as much time staying with her and Ken at their farm as possible. I have a busy schedule at the best of times, with two walking tours a year and always a book on the boil, not to mention my own garden and family. However it became obvious to me that I could be of tremendous assistance, not just in a physical or practical sense, but in being able to lift the mood of the household and provide some on-the-spot respite for Ken, who is gradually recovering from his own medical problems. David has been fantastically supportive of my desire to spend time in Canada because he understands my deep emotional connection with my sister.

From my perspective I am grateful that I am able to go and help as often as I can. I try to go for six to eight weeks at a time, several times a year. In the not-too-distant future I will probably just go and stay indefinitely. My belief is that my sister had a pretty poor start to her life. Her mother's death, her alcoholic father and the distressing atmosphere of her family home forced her to virtually run away as soon as she was able. As her only sister, I feel if I can help to make this part of her life a little happier or more comfortable and secure, then I will do everything in my power to do so.

23

By the time my cookbook was nearly finished, I was concerned about Margaret's deteriorating condition. I had regular phone conversations with Ken at the weekends, and also exchanged emails with Margaret's best friend, Fran, another teacher who had travelled with her to Canada in the 1960s. Both of them warned me I would be shocked when I saw my sister again, that she had lost a lot of cognitive function and had started suffering from anxiety, a normal factor in advanced Alzheimer's cases.

Here it was, late October, and so much had happened my in life and in hers. I was apprehensive but also looking forward to seeing Margaret and Ken again and getting a handle on the situation. I spotted them immediately as I came through the arrival doors at the airport – Ken is very tall and stands head and shoulders above the crowd. Margaret was by his side, looking pale and slightly troubled. I threw my arms around them both and made eye contact with her. It was obvious to me that at that precise moment she had absolutely no idea who I was. Her puzzlement could no longer be disguised.

It was amazing that Ken had continued coping at home with Margaret's illness. He had begun taking her two times a week to a daycentre for dementia sufferers, and that gave him a brief respite from her round-the-clock care. Margaret was less and less able to help with the basic food preparation for their evening meal, so they now went out to dinner sometimes three or four times a week. Family members and friends invited them over for meals on a regular basis, but it was becoming increasingly tricky because Margaret found it almost impossible to sit at a dining table waiting for a meal to be served. She was restless and anxious, and required medication to settle her down when she became agitated.

Since my departure the previous Christmas, a series of trained carers had been coming to the house to help bathe Margaret, start the dinner and manage a few household chores. This set my mind at rest somewhat, knowing that Ken was getting support and that Margaret was so well looked after. She had gained weight since my last visit and was looking a little neater and tidier. I realised that before the carers came on the scene she had probably not been showering or washing her clothes very often, and that routine grooming tasks such as nail clipping and hair cutting had been beyond her.

The carers were warm and efficient. I decided it would be a good idea to follow them as they worked with Margaret, to pick up tips on the best way of managing her. It's very confronting for a proud, independent woman to suddenly need help getting into a bath or to dress, and I didn't want to offend her or overstep the mark. Up until now, my relationship with my sister had been affectionate but not intimate. I realised the time had arrived to step over the line and take a different role as one of her carers, and I was more than a little apprehensive.

The first night the carer arrived while I was cooking dinner. These days Margaret wanted to get into bed almost as soon as the meal was finished, as she could no longer sit and relax in front of the television. The bedroom was her refuge. So after dinner I followed Margaret and the carer down the hallway to get organised for a bath. While the hot water was cascading into the deep spa in the ensuite we started looking through the drawers for some clean pyjamas. Each drawer was in a state of disarray. There were handbags and unopened mail in the sock drawer, and shoes in the underwear drawer, and when we finally found the drawer containing nighties we also uncovered a cat bowl full of mouldy cat food. I couldn't help laughing, although the implications were frightening. The chest of drawers reflected Margaret's total confusion. I realised I would need to start sorting through her personal effects to try to restore at least some semblance of order. I took it upon myself to sort through her cupboards and wardrobes on the mornings when she was at the daycentre, and it was also agreed that I should get her into a hot bath at least four times a week.

After her relaxing hot bath, Margaret fell happily into bed and was asleep within moments. I joined Ken in the family room, watching television, and he updated me on Margaret's circumstances. They had seen a specialist several times who at the last visit had recommended increasing Margaret's daily dose of a medication that helped cognitive function. However her agitation was intensifying and the specialist wanted to prescribe various drugs to calm her down. To sedate her. Ken deeply opposed the idea of drugging Margaret to make her docile. This had always been one of his main objections against sending her into a care facility. He had visited a few such homes, and every time he was confronted by patients sitting, passive, staring vacantly into space, apparently drugged to the eyeballs. He also knew in his heart that Margaret simply wouldn't be happy living away from home, and that she would become even more confused and anxious.

'I know she would hate it, and so would I,' he said. 'I'd be lonely here without her. I'd really miss her.'

I had to do whatever was possible to help Ken achieve his aim of keeping Margaret at home for as long as possible. I realised that inevitably it would become unsustainable, but I had no idea when that moment would arrive. Until you have walked down the path of

Alzheimer's, it's difficult not to find such uncertainty daunting, but after a while, it becomes normal.

As Ken and I chatted, Margaret suddenly appeared in the doorway, bright as a button. Her face was still so expressive, with her large green eyes and captivating smile. She joined us for a few moments, then wandered away again. Back to bed. Then up again for another wander. Once or twice she emerged with several layers of daytime clothes over her pyjamas. Two pairs of slacks and three cardigans. I gently persuaded her to peel off the layers and coaxed her back to bed.

I discovered the pattern of their nights together. Ken would fall asleep in his big recliner chair in front of the television. Margaret would get up and down restlessly and come looking for him. Eventually he would go to bed, usually after midnight, and she would settle for a couple of hours and then start wandering again. His sleep was constantly disturbed by her night ramblings, and they both got their best rest after 6 am. I rose early, but let them sleep late. Their closeness was very touching.

Twice a week, we dropped Margaret at the daycentre. I used this free time to do some more work on the final edit of the cookbook and try to restore some order around the house. One day, Ken and I spent three hours doing nothing but sifting through her things; it was quite an adventure uncovering bits and pieces she had filed and hidden away in strange places for years. There were small bundles of cash and mail that had never been opened and cheques that had never been presented at the bank. There were household items from the kitchen cupboards and even an empty wineglass with the traces of a good red. It was at the back of the sock drawer. There were letters from friends, letters from me, half-eaten bags of sweets, and a few sketches done on one of the art group days. I felt as though I was invading her personal space, stepping into her private bewilderment.

I also went through the wardrobe. Margaret always preferred very plain, good-quality blouses, slacks and jumpers. She's not a frilly girl at all, and owns very few dresses or high-heeled shoes. I realised most of the clothes hadn't been washed in quite some time. They were not dirty, as such, just rather stale-smelling where they had been worn and hung again at night. I gradually washed every item, discarding those that were frayed or had holes; I made small repairs and replaced lost buttons. I enjoyed setting her clothes to rights. It was satisfying and I also somehow felt a connection with her through the lovely things she wore. It was as though I was gaining a greater insight into my sister, who she was and what her life had been like all those years before we met again.

The carers didn't work weekends, so we decided it would be a good idea if I gave Margaret her regular bath. Even though she had always preferred to take a shower, the carers had discovered that the hot water really soothed her. I ran a bath in the ensuite adjoining my bedroom rather than in the deep spa. I filled the tub with hot water sprinkled with fragrant oils and then went looking for Margaret, who was wandering yet again. When I suggested a bath she looked unimpressed.

'I don't need a bath. I had one this morning.' She hadn't, of course.

'But I've already run the bath. I'd hate to waste the water.'

'Oh all right then, if I must.'

Margaret undressed with some difficulty, then I helped her step into the bath. As she slipped beneath the steaming water she let out a deep sigh. She put her head back and closed her eyes and I gently washed her arms and legs, massaging them to help the oils soak into her skin, which looked rather dry.

'Isn't this lovely,' she said, opening her eyes and looking at me sweetly. 'Do you have someone nice to do this for you at home?'

It was such a tender moment. The intimacy of helping her let go of her troubles, even if just for a few precious moments.

I knew that she often felt fretful and worried. That her anxiety was a result of her confusion and her knowledge that she was losing her grip on the real world.

Just imagine living in a world that has no reality. Where commonplace things become meaningless and nothing makes any sense. It's a very frightening world and the most awful part is that you know something is dreadfully wrong and you just can't work out what it is.

This is Margaret's world. She's still inside there somewhere, the real Margaret. The whole Margaret. She's trapped inside a brain that simply doesn't work anymore.

I smoothed a warm, wet washer over her forehead.

'Just relax, Margaret. Everything is fine. Everything is OK. There's nothing to worry about.'

While I was in Canada, two major events occurred back home. The Australian government changed overnight, in general elections that I was sad to miss. I love election night, even if the voting goes against my particular political beliefs. This was the first time I had been out of the country for a federal poll, and I cursed missing out on a good party with the television going strong and lots of lively debate about the swings and voting trends. David kept me posted, and so did Miriam. There were 3 am calls and lots of texts and emails as the results came pouring in.

The other big event was David's Raymond Longford Award. It's the highest accolade the Australian Film Institute can bestow on an individual for their contribution to screen culture, named in honour of one of Australia's great filmmaking pioneers. For my husband this was the highlight of his career, and of course he was deeply disappointed that I wouldn't be able to fly to Melbourne to be with him on the big night. Although it was to be televised in Australia, I wouldn't be able to see him receive his award, or hear his acceptance speech. I was disappointed. But he took Aaron along, and it was a great bonding moment for them.

I encouraged Ken to take advantage of my presence in Canada to take some time for himself; to go to local agricultural meetings and to socialise with friends and family away from the pressures of caring for Margaret. He had an invitation to the annual dinner of his late father's army regiment, a very male-oriented gathering that he has always enjoyed attending. He looked dashing when he came down the hall from the bedroom, dressed to the nines in a black dinner suit, highly polished shoes, a bow tie and a white silk scarf. Margaret looked amazed to see her husband dressed so elegantly. I took a photograph of them together.

The next day he presented me with a copy of the evening's menu. It is traditional to serve game at this particular regimental dinner. Local game food. I was appalled when I realised what they had eaten. I thought it was the most bizarre, hilarious and politically incorrect meal I could ever imagine:

Salmon, mussel and deer sausage chowder
Bison meat pie with tomato jam and mushy peas
Chanterelle stuffed cougar with arugula and parmesan salad
Slow-roasted venison steak with chestnut puree
Moose roast with Yorkshire pudding
Kiwifruit sorbet (Ken provides the fruit from his orchard)
Cheese and coffee

My seven-week stay in Canada passed all too quickly, a lovely time in many ways, but worrying. I was concerned about future care for both Margaret and Ken. He had been diagnosed with a form of cancer; the treatment made him feel weak and lethargic. I could easily see them getting into difficulty unless some more permanent help was put in place.

One of the women in Margaret's art group told us that she employed a full-time live-in carer for her mother, who was in her nineties and no longer able to care for herself. The assistance was organised through a scheme supported by the Canadian government. Workers trained in geriatric care were brought in from the Philippines under a two-year contract; they worked six days a week, lived on the premises, and were around in the wee small hours of the morning if there was an urgent problem.

Ken made inquiries and put his name on a register of people wanting to contract a carer. It would take three to four months for a suitable person to be matched to Margaret's needs. In my view it wasn't the perfect solution, but it was certainly better than the existing arrangements.

I left for home less than a week before Christmas, promising to return as soon as I could manage it. I knew that Ken had become dependent on me for emotional support, partly because I managed to lift the mood in the house, introducing some extra warmth and humour. When I was not around Margaret was inclined to go into her shell, to stop talking much and to sleep more. I could see that my presence in their home was greatly needed, but I also knew that my work and family commitments made it difficult to spend more than a few weeks at a time away from home. Once again I felt torn. For years, it's been a tug of love between France and Australia, between my village house in Frayssinet, and David and the farm. Now I was being pulled three ways. My sister and her doting husband needed me more than I had really been needed by anyone for many years. I laughed to myself, remembering the sense of freedom I had experienced when I first escaped from responsibility and lived alone in France for those heady six months. Here I was, seven years later, very much in demand and no longer the free spirit I had planned to be.

24

Over the past few years our Christmas celebrations have become more frenetic as family numbers have swelled and the time I have available for planning, shopping and preparation is more limited. This Christmas was no exception. I landed back in Australia knowing it would be a rush to get organised.

Realistically I only had two days left to purchase the food, to buy gifts, and to decorate the tree. But even though I was doing all the shopping in Bathurst, and not going down to Sydney, I managed without a drama. We have abandoned exchanging presents between the adults – there are just too many of us – and concentrate on catering for the children. This made my task easier. I always start by buying every child a book and go from there, checking with their parents to avoid doubling up with someone else.

This would be the first time Miriam, Rick and the boys would not be coming to the farm for Christmas. They were living separately, of course, and Miriam didn't have a reliable car for the long drive. Airfares for five people were out of the question. Aaron and Lorna were also coming separately, and these changes in marital relations made life a bit more complicated. My brother, Jon, always comes down from northern

New South Wales and stays for two or three days, and this year my other brother, Dan, who lives in Bathurst, would also come out to the farm and stay overnight. Ethan, Lynne and their two would drive over from the Mountains. And Tony and Simone were coming from Sydney. So it would be a pretty full table, as usual.

I must admit to feeling more than a little sad, however, that Miriam and our grandsons would not be with us. Apart from last year, when I stayed with Margaret and Ken, we had always spent our Christmases together. Just as I loved being woken by my own overexcited children at the crack of dawn on Christmas morning, so I derived huge pleasure from seeing the excitement in the eyes of my grandchildren. David has always thought our celebrations over the top, but for me it's such a happy time of year and an excuse to spoil the kids and overindulge in food and wine.

This year we were having our celebratory meal on Christmas Eve, in the European fashion. This had been decided for practical reasons, because early on Boxing Day I had to drive to Sydney to start work on a five-day-a-week radio show for the ABC. I realised that if I cooked our usual hot lunch on Christmas Day, I would probably end up feeling tired and frazzled, and I needed to be fresh and relaxed for the show.

It seems that every Christmas has its own drama attached to it. Two years ago, while cooking the lunch, I set fire to a tray of duck fat that was heating in the wood stove, and our smoke-filled kitchen was invaded by uniformed men from the local bushfire brigade. It was pandemonium. In fact, looking back over the years I can recall one hysterical incident after another...

The year Miriam was carrying a bowl of cooked pet food out to the fridge in the garage to make room in the kitchen fridge, and accidentally bumped into the door jamb (I believe a dog was jumping up trying to get at the food). The bowl split neatly in half, slicing a deep gash in her wrist that required a mad dash to the hospital and more than a dozen stitches.

The year my brother, Jon, threw a bone into the garden and our sooky springer spaniel, Spot, lunged for it at the same moment as Jon's Staffordshire bull terrier. The terrier latched onto the spaniel's loose cheeks and ripped the flesh apart – again there was blood everywhere. On that occasion I called our local GP, who sutured the wound while sipping on a cold beer.

The year I removed the muzzle from Miriam's Jack Russell terrier after lunch, and he promptly slunk off and massacred two of our ducks. The sight of David running through the paddock holding aloft two ducks dripping with blood and shouting angrily is one I don't think our grandchildren will ever forget. And so it goes on.

This year was no exception, except that the dogs were a bit better behaved. I was cooking the enormous turkey in the electric oven and, as usual, had the wood stove going for the roasted vegetables. As one of the children walked past it, the electric stove sent out a blinding flash and promptly exploded – a thin wisp of black smoke emerged from the back. We all got a terrible fright, but fortunately no one was injured. As it was Christmas Eve I feared that it would be impossible to find an electrician, but miraculously we managed to track down a cheerful bloke who agreed to drive out from town and have a look.

Eventually the oven was working again, and the meal went ahead without another hitch. The dramas that punctuate our family Christmas get-togethers have amusement value but, quite frankly, I could do without them given that the day is fraught with activity and large numbers of overexcited children and probably far too much champagne and red wine. One year, perhaps, David and I may just go out to a smart restaurant for lunch and I can relax and let someone else do all the work. On second thought, it's highly unlikely!

Over January, ABC Radio allows its regular presenters to take a long break, which gives the network a chance to try out new program ideas and presenters. Libbi Gorr has done quite a bit of work over the years filling in as a guest presenter, and it was she who suggested to the ABC's programmers that together we would make a good combination on air. The idea of two women presenting a show was a bit of a novelty, and they went for it. We had already had a brief try-out when the regular evening presenter on ABC Radio's 702 channel, James O'Loughlin, was unable to do his show. Without notice we jumped in, and it had seemed to work. The chemistry between us was good and we tried to create a show which was lively and entertaining.

Our summer program ran from seven until ten o'clock in the evenings, Monday to Friday. Traditionally the first hour has always been a quiz with audience participation, and since the quiz is one of the timeslot's most popular fixtures, we decided not to fiddle with it too much for fear of alienating the loyal audience.

The content of the next two hours was open to us. We wanted to have a mixture of light and more serious interviews, throwing together everything from arts to politics and socially relevant themes. It was fun coming up with ideas, but also a lot of hard work. We had a smart producer to help us, but every day we burned through four or five ideas an hour. We wanted the show to be fast-paced and a bit quirky. One of the main problems was finding interesting people to interview in January. So many Australians are away on holidays at that time of year, and it proved to be a logistical nightmare finding 'talking heads' to discuss the topics we were sourcing from local and interstate newspapers. As a cost saving, the January shows are broadcast nationally, and that further complicated matters. Perth was three hours behind us in Sydney, which meant that Perth listeners couldn't phone in for the quiz, or make comments when we called for listener feedback. The ABC doesn't like national shows to appear Sydney-centric so we never mentioned that we were broadcasting from the corporation's studios in Ultimo.

Libbi and I have very different presenting styles, and this, I suspect, gave our shows a certain charm. She always asks left-of-centre questions, while I'm much more pragmatic and straightforward. We tend to make each other laugh a lot, and this can be dangerous. One night, I slipped some rather risqué questions into the quiz, and Libbi was unprepared for them. She started to laugh and had to turn off her microphone as tears poured down her face. I tried to keep the show bouncing along until she recovered. The next day an ABC manager gave me a light rap over the knuckles, and reminded me that at 7 pm many children are still listening. I toned it down for the rest of our time on air.

One of the things I loved about radio was that we didn't have to spend hours being primped and preened by make-up artists and wardrobe people like we did for our TV show – we could turn up in daggy clothes without a dash of mascara or lipstick on, and the audience would be none the wiser. We could also choose our own content and interview subjects, steering away from the trivial topics that we so often found ourselves having to discuss on *The Catch-Up*. The immediacy of radio is so compelling. Being able to talk back and forth with the audience throughout the show was very stimulating: listeners often had such amazing thoughts and experiences to share. No celebrities required!

25

Just as motherhood defined my sense of self in the decades from my twenties to forties, so becoming a grandmother has enriched my life over the past fourteen years. I know a young woman who had a child in her twenties and her mother refused to take on the role of grandmother.

'People think differently about you when they know you're a grandmother. They think less of you . . . they think you're old,' she said.

I have the reverse view. I am delighted to have this gaggle of small children in my life and I mention them to all and sundry whenever I get an opportunity. I don't whip out dozens of photographs and bore people to death, but I love recounting funny anecdotes about my relationship with the children and their relationships with each other. They are all so different and yet they also have so much in common. Nothing makes them happier than to all be together at the same time, at the farm, being cousins.

Caius, the youngest, talks about 'the cousins' constantly. Whenever he comes out to Yetholme he asks if any of the cousins will be there and is crestfallen if I say they're not around. I have printed out photographs of them all together, playing, and put them up on the wall in the family room so that in between visits he can be reminded of the fun they had last time.

In January, while I was still doing the radio show, Miriam managed to get up to the farm with the boys and one weekend we were able to have a full family reunion with all the children and their parents. They wanted Christmas again, of course, so I bought another ham and cooked a turkey for Sunday lunch. The children climbed the huge old cypress tree out the front and galloped around the paddocks like free spirits. It's snake time of year in this district so they must all wear long pants and boots before stepping off the verandah. The woodland part of the farm has suffered greatly from the long drought and several of the older trees – probably more than two hundred years old – have simply toppled over because of dryness around their root systems. This has made the woodland an extremely dangerous place and I have banned the children from playing there, which is a shame because it was always one of their favourite haunts. I love the fact that, when they are here, they are outdoors much more than inside. I ban daytime TV unless it's raining and I often pack them a picnic lunch and send them off on an adventure.

Miriam and I were now communicating much more effectively and she seemed, slowly, to be getting back on her feet after what had obviously been a very difficult year for her, managing a lot of the time on her own. The boys had been spending forty percent of their time with Rick and the rest with their mother; Rick and Miriam had worked out a schedule that suited them both and seemed to work quite well for the children.

As a mother and grandmother, I had to think carefully about my role in all of this. There was no point expecting Miriam – or indeed any of our children – to behave, react and make decisions in the exact way that I would have in the same circumstances. It's easy to maintain happy accord with adult children when things are going smoothly, and it's only when a spanner (such as separation and divorce) is thrown into the works that these relationships can become strained. I knew that I wanted to retain my affectionate bond with my ex-son-in-law and ex-daughter-in-law, but also that I needed to offer unconditional love, support and acceptance of my children and their choices – while supporting my grandchildren through it all as best as I could.

One aspect of this new arrangement which I found curious was that Miriam was now able to lead a double life. For part of each week she was a full-time single mother with a lot of responsibility on her shoulders. Up early getting the children moving for school; organising their uniforms and breakfasts and packing their sandwiches for lunchtime. After school it's homework and music practice, dinner and bedtime.

During the weekdays and weekends when their father had the children, Miriam could revert to being a single girl again. She had lopped her long curly locks and now had a brilliant blonde cap. She had lost weight, as many of us do during times of emotional stress, and was wearing more outrageous clothes than she had since her days at university. I found this change a bit unsettling but I realised that she needed to find herself again. To re-establish herself as a sexy, gorgeous young woman. She couldn't just sit at home feeling sad and sorry for herself, and by all appearances she had no intention of doing so. She was out there in the wide world, reconnecting with her school and university friends on Facebook and My Space, and meeting new and interesting people. Miriam's quest for momentary freedom from responsibility mirrors my own escape to France back in 2000. It's just that she's only thirty-five and I was turning fifty when I took the plunge. I tried not to be alarmed but it worried me, this new way her generation had found to interact. It was a whole new world to me and I had to keep reminding myself to embrace the new. Accept the changes. Go with the flow. The boys had learned to be much more independent and when I visited them in April I was impressed at how organised and self-sufficient they had become in the last twelve months. Without two adults to care for them at once they had to develop skills and take on responsibilities. That in itself is never a bad thing.

Nevertheless, I challenged her a little, and while visiting I put forward the theory that she was actually enjoying this new arrangement. That single life had certain benefits. She could be a mum and enjoy all the pleasures of raising a family of bright boys without the complication of also having a husband to deal with; then she could be an independent, single girl for a few days and rediscover her younger self.

She smiled and agreed with me. She's having a lot of fun.

Back at the farm, when I was visited by Lorna and her kids one weekend, I tried my theory on her. Perhaps she too was enjoying handing the children over to their dad and heading out for a few nights of freedom.

'Is it like this for you too?' I asked.

'Not really,' she replied. 'At first I loved the freedom but these days I often feel lonely even when I have the children. After they have gone to bed I'm on my own and it's not really all that much fun.'

I've realised that listening and offering support rather than judgement or even advice is fundamental to keeping the family together after these major life changes. Whatever I do, I must not impose my desire for the status quo. I must move on, as they have done.

26

In April, my cookbook was released, and I was caught up in a whirlwind book tour around the eastern states. *The Long Table* was a departure for me, as I'd never written an entire book about food before, or had the opportunity to share my family's favourite recipes in print. I love book tours, and this time I was speaking at a series of lunches and dinners where the restaurant kitchens had prepared meals from the book. The first event was at a very swish restaurant at Balmoral Beach, where I grew up. The restaurant is located in what was once our bathing pavilion, where we changed into and out of our swimming costumes just about every day in summer. It was a local crowd and I had a great time recounting food stories and memories from my childhood. It was pure nostalgia.

The tour had been divided in two because I had to break into it with a trek in the Himalayas which had been organised for more than a year. This time we were heading for a state in northern India known as Sikkhim, which is famous for its diversity of flora and forests of rhododendrons, then to Bhutan, a mysterious small kingdom that I had read about often, but never visited.

For the first time ever on one of my treks, it rained heavily, and this

155

made the climbing conditions cold and miserable. We were looking for rhododendrons but the mountain we were ascending was entirely shrouded in thick, damp mist. I had expected impressive scenery but this was like walking through pea soup. By the time we reached our summit, at an elevation of 4500 metres, the group appeared exhausted, damp and dispirited. We curled up in our tents very early. Just before sunrise I woke suddenly, hearing the bells of yaks as they wandered through camp. I poked my head out of the tent flap and behold, we were surrounded by the most spectacular snow-peaked mountains, with banks of rhododendrons beside us. Without hesitation I ran along the line of tents, waking up my sleeping trekkers. They emerged slowly, but their grumpiness evaporated when they saw where we were. The fog had lifted, the clouds had departed, and we had a 360-degree view. It was worth the aching legs and altitude headaches, we all agreed over a breakfast of hot oatmeal and omelettes.

In June, after the trek and the book tour were over, I felt a need to return to Canada to see how Margaret and Ken were faring. I could never have predicted my relationship with them would work out this way. I came back into Margaret's life as a rather eager younger sister, keen to re-establish a bond and to find out more about her journey over the last fifty years. Now I was a critical part of her support system during a long and devastating illness. Every time I went back I was apprehensive about how much further her condition would have deteriorated and how Ken would be coping. Yet I also had a strong sense of coming home. The spare room had become 'my' room and I left behind some of my clothes and books and toiletries between visits.

The flight from Vancouver to the island was delayed because the airline was waiting for a late connecting plane from Toronto that had eight passengers scheduled on our leg of the journey. My mobile phone wouldn't kick in and, waiting on the tarmac, there was no way I could let Ken know of this last-minute hold up. I was worried sick about him hanging around at the other end, trying to cope with Margaret.

Eventually, more than an hour later, we took off. Sure enough, when I saw Ken in the arrivals hall he was looking extremely frazzled. There was no sign of Margaret. She had been unable to sit still and wait for my arrival, and she was pacing frantically up and down, gazing out of windows and looking very agitated. I went to hug her but she was just too upset to respond. She needed to go home, back to her safe and familiar environment. Strange places had now become alien and frightening, and crowds of people were an impossibility for her.

Of course, this is why Alzheimer's patients are seldom seen out and about in the community. Their nervous and irrational behaviour is deemed anti-social and they are kept away from the public gaze, partly for their own wellbeing, but also because of the embarrassment of dealing with their erratic demeanour. It was immediately obvious to me that Margaret had gone downhill considerably. While she looked physically very healthy, her eyes were filled with panic and confusion. Ken just looked exhausted. I felt desperately sorry for them both.

Back at their farm, we settled Margaret down with a sedative and shared a simple late dinner. Ken told me that they couldn't really go to restaurants any more because Margaret became impossibly restless. She would pace and try sitting down at other people's tables and picking up food from their plates. He needed six arms and legs to manage her. He was now on a form of chemotherapy and had very little energy. He had managed, however, to clean out his home office in order to make a large, comfortable bedroom for the carer from the Philippines who was scheduled to arrive in the near future. In my view, she couldn't get here soon enough.

This was my saddest and most painful visit so far. Margaret could no longer be dropped at the daycentre on her own. She grew far too agitated after Ken left and would try to escape, which could be extremely dangerous. She needed one-on-one attention; she required regular medication to calm her down and she now needed help going to the toilet. One of her carers, Bev, had been taking Margaret to the centre, but I was more than happy to be her supporter while I was there, as daunting as the prospect was.

The aim of the centre was to provide respite for the families of dementia patients, and to help fill the sufferers' day with occupational therapy, some gentle exercise and relaxation, and a good hot lunch. The staff who ran it took a very positive approach, encouraging their clients to dwell on the cognitive function they still had rather than worrying or getting anxious about their diminished memories. Being so closely involved with Margaret over the last couple of years I can clearly see how aware she is that something is happening to her. I had always thought that people with dementia didn't suffer because they were blissfully unaware of their deterioration. Nothing could be further from the truth. Margaret definitely knows that her world is shrinking and her defence has been to withdraw, to say as little as possible and to desperately try to cling to some sense of normalcy.

Ken dropped us at the centre and we sat around a large table with twelve others, including some volunteer helpers and the trained support staff. The daily newspapers were spread out and morning tea was served, with toast. The team leader read pieces from the newspaper then encouraged discussion. The idea was to keep bringing the real world back into their clients' lives. Some of the group were very vocal and still quite capable of conversation. Some sat very quietly and seldom spoke. There were equal numbers of men and women; their ages varied dramatically. Some people appeared to be in their late eighties but three or four were relatively young – perhaps in their late fifties or early sixties. Sometimes they seemed able to relate to each other, sometimes they disappeared back into their own worlds. We went for a walk after morning tea then came back and played a game of boules, sitting in plastic chairs and directing the balls into the centre of a circle.

Lunchtime was difficult. Margaret could still feed herself but she was inclined to help herself to other people's drinks or lunge for food from their plates. Not all of them were understanding. She also tried to bite into objects on the table. Each client had a painted pet rock with their name on it – obviously from one of the occupational therapy sessions – and this was used to mark their places at the table. Margaret tried eating hers and I noticed just in time; it could easily crack one of her front teeth. While waiting for the lunch to be served she also tried to devour a small bunch of flowers in the centre of the table. One of the other clients filled her pockets with cutlery, while another had to be coaxed to eat anything at all.

After lunch, a volunteer with a guitar and a bundle of sheet music arrived to entertain the group for an hour. He played old popular songs and everyone was encouraged to sing along or to get up and dance if they were so inclined. Margaret was mostly quiet until they started singing 'Waltzing Matilda'. She joined in with a big grin – I was told she did so every week.

Spending a few days at the centre added to my understanding of the progress of dementia. It was sad to see how these gentle people had been affected and how it had completely changed their lives. It was still possible to detect their individual characters and personalities, and it was tough knowing that it was downhill all the way. No chance of a remission, let alone a cure. I can't help but worry about what the future holds for my lovely sister.

Ken had organised for the Alzheimer's specialist to visit during my stay so that I would have an opportunity to ask questions. It was pointless having a consultation in his office as he wouldn't be able to assess Margaret properly. He needed to sit for an hour and observe her in her own environment. This made a lot of sense to me.

He arrived with a laptop and made himself at home in the main living room, taking notes as we both gave him our views of how Margaret was managing. She was acutely aware that we were discussing her and this seemed to make her even more anxious and agitated than usual. She tried participating in the conversation but couldn't sit still for long enough, and looked nervously around the room from one of us to the other. Her powers of speech were now quite limited, and when she tried to contribute she was left grasping for the right words. The sense of frustration and powerlessness on her face was heartbreaking.

The doctor recommended that we try a new and much more powerful medication to control her fretfulness. He suggested we double her daily dose of anti-anxiety tablets, and wanted to prescribe a powerful sedative at bedtime to try to prevent her night-time wanderings, along with another drug that he believed would stabilise her mood swings. It was true that since I last visited she had become much more difficult to manage. She was not aggressive but she certainly resisted getting up in the morning, and sometimes she actually wrestled with us, not wanting to be directed to the toilet or into the bath. One morning, when she was particularly upset, she turned on me in the bathroom and put up two fists as if she wanted to fight. I almost laughed aloud in disbelief, then she somehow realised what she was doing and capitulated, meekly allowing me to undress her and help her into the tub of hot water.

I asked the specialist what we should expect over the next twelve months. How would the disease progress and what signs and symptoms should we be looking out for? He told us there was no timeframe for Alzheimer's, and that each patient deteriorated at a different rate. However, he reminded us that Margaret was already at an advanced stage and said that we should anticipate a steep decline over the next year. Eventually, she would simply not be able to get out of bed and walk any more – not because she didn't have the strength in her legs, but because her brain would have stopped sending messages to her limbs. Her entire system would gradually shut down and she would slip into a coma.

We had to take Margaret to her GP to get the prescriptions recommended by the specialist. Once again she was aware that she was the focus of the conversation and I got rather annoyed with the doctor who persisted in talking about her as though she wasn't there at all. He gave her no credit for comprehension.

The first morning of the new regime Margaret was knocked around very badly by the new drugs. I googled them on the internet and was alarmed to read about them in more detail. One of the drugs was designed to treat patients with schizophrenia, and it had some pretty nasty side effects. For Margaret the impact was immediate: she couldn't stay awake. She retreated back to bed and slept almost all day long. I managed to get some lunch into her, but she was so spaced out that it was almost impossible to get her to do anything. I decided to keep a diary to chart the effects of the drugs over the next two weeks.

At the end of the fortnight I rang the GP who had given us the prescriptions recommended by the specialist and read him some of the notes from my detailed diary. Magarets's intense lethargy had worn off after a few days, but the overall effect from my perspective was that Margaret's abilities had gone backwards, quite sharply. She had become incontinent, had stopped even attempting to speak and was having great difficulty walking, negotiating stairs and even getting into and out of the car. Ken and I agreed that instead of making Margaret's life easier and our task as carers less difficult, if anything the medication had made things worse. It had, literally, turned her into a zombie. I was greatly relieved when the doctor suggested dropping the new tablets, though he wanted us to stick to the double dose of calming pills and also the evening medication to help her sleep.

Through this experience I realised just how important it is for people in Margaret's situation to have an advocate. The doctors and the specialists really had no concept of what it was like to live with Alzheimer's twenty-four hours a day, seven days a week. They might see patients on a regular basis and visit them in nursing homes and other care facilities, but it is the families and the full-time carers who really have a sense of how the sufferer is faring. We knew that Margaret was still very aware of her surroundings and that she understood a great deal of what was going on around her and what was being said. She had not, as some people suggested, reverted to infancy. Part of me was angry about all this. The foolish assumptions of people who really didn't understand. Like Margaret I felt frustrated. But I was not powerless, and I would continue to fight on her behalf.

27

Margaret's carer from the Philippines was due to arrive and I had concerns about how it would all work out. At this stage Margaret didn't readily warm to new people and she could be tricky to manage if she decided not to cooperate. Getting her out of bed involved literally flicking the covers away before she had time to react and swinging her legs onto the floor while in the same instant lifting her upwards onto her feet. The idea is to get her moving in one smooth action. Her local carer, Bev, developed this technique and it usually worked, although not always for me. Sometimes Margaret would grab onto the blankets and hang on for grim death. I always left her to relax for a while before making another attempt. I hated to feel I was battling her, but I also knew it was vital to get her up and moving in the mornings.

Fedema was the name of our new carer, and she arrived with the woman from the agency that facilitated this live-in arrangement. Fedema was very small and had a wonderful open face with a wide smile. We had a cup of tea and I quickly discovered a lot about her education and training for this job.

In the Philippines, all schooling – infants, primary and high school – is conducted in the English language. The government has known for decades that their greatest export asset is their people, and they have been supplying workers for a wide range of practical and caring jobs overseas for more than fifty years. The Filipino government identifies where the overseas job opportunities lie and then helps to train and educate its workers accordingly. In Canada, there is a tremendous lack of trained geriatric carers willing to put in the hours to support elderly and frail people who want to remain living at home. To qualify for the scheme, Fedema has been required to spend at least two years working with a family that includes an elderly person in need of care. In her case this involved moving to Hong Kong to live in with a family of five – middle-aged parents, two teenage children and a grandmother in a wheelchair. As she described this period of training I realised that it must have been tremendously difficult for her. She was not simply a carer but the household domestic, doing all the shopping, cooking, cleaning and laundry while also taking care of her elderly charge.

Ken had signed Fedema up on a two-year contract. She would live in with full board and pay for her six-day week. After the agency representative departed we did our best to make her feel welcome, showing her the room that had been so carefully prepared for her and giving her a guided tour of the house and garden. Fedema was obviously keen for this arrangement to work. She immediately made herself as useful as possible and I warmed to her, although Margaret was a little less than enthusiastic. Ken and I made it clear from the outset that caring for Margaret should be her number-one priority. Housework and laundry came very low down on our list of requirements.

I saw my role as teaching Fedema everything she needed to know to make the transition as smooth as possible. I was to go home in a few weeks and I hoped she would have settled in by the time I left. We chatted amiably as we got on with the various tasks at hand and I discovered that she had left behind a husband and four children in the Philippines. She proudly showed me a photograph of her lovely family. The children ranged in age from three to ten.

I could barely contain my dismay. It should have been obvious but it hadn't occurred to me. Fedema was making an enormous sacrifice, living without her husband and children for two years, to try to improve their lives by gaining Canadian residency. She told me that two other family members had done the same thing, and both of these women now lived happily in Vancouver. Neither of them had children to leave behind, but they too had been through this same trial period before being accepted into the country.

I was very troubled by the situation. I knew full well that Ken could only keep Margaret at home if she had a live-in carer. And I also appreciated that this might well be Fedema's best chance at making a new life for her family in a more affluent society. Yet it seemed a tragedy to me that the world worked this way. A woman from a Third World country had to leave behind her precious children so that people in a wealthy country could have affordable aged care. I was appalled and deeply saddened, and that night in bed I wept not only for my sister but also for Fedema, even though she seemed so happy to have this opportunity. It was not lost on me that she had already been away from her children for two years, in Hong Kong, before she came to us.

From the first day Fedema fitted into the family and exceeded our expectations, although there were some interesting adjustments to make. I hadn't anticipated that she would never have cooked European meals, and while we all loved Asian food, Fedema needed to learn the basics of some simple meals that Ken and Margaret are more accustomed to eating. I started by teaching her to make chicken soup with vegetables and then shepherd's pie and sausages with onion gravy. She was used to eating rice three times a day so I tried to include several rice dishes along the way. We stocked the shelves with chilli sauce and various Asian condiments so she could prepare some of her own favourite meals as well. One night I roasted a chicken with bacon and bread stuffing and lots of crispy baked potatoes and gravy. Fedema loved this, and wrote down every step in great detail so she could prepare the same meal for the family after I left. She also enthusiastically offered to assist Ken in planting out his spring vegetable garden and helped me weed the ornamental garden I had planted with bulbs and perennials to give Margaret some cheer. Fedema had never gardened before, but took to it immediately. Indeed she was willing to do anything and everything to help, and her attitude was unfailingly positive and supportive. I could tell that her presence would make a tremendous difference.

28

David learned to operate a computer less than five years ago, and before that time he relied on various production assistants or members of his family (mainly me) to type his correspondence for him. So I was tremendously relieved when he decided to master keyboard skills. It lifted a burden from my shoulders and also made him much more independent, running his filmmaking business from home. Communicating by email has in fact made life easier for us both, given that we both travel so much and spend so many months of the year apart.

Initially, David's emails to me were very brief and to the point because his typing was still very slow and laboured, but gradually he gained speed and confidence and long messages seem to flow effortlessly from his computer into mine. While I was with Ken and Margaret it was wonderful for me to have someone to talk to about the difficulties I was experiencing in dealing with the situation. I usually waited until the evenings, after Margaret was settled, to write to him about how the day had gone. In particular I needed to express my feelings – the sadness I felt, the fears I had for the future and the pain of coping with a state of affairs that was only going to get worse as time went on:

The new medication makes a tremendous difference but it's quite brutal – what Ken was dreading. A 'subdued' wife. Easier for all of us BUT! This afternoon I lost her for a few minutes – I tried not to panic. Then I found her sitting, knees tucked under her chin, on the cold tiled floor of her old art studio. She looked frightened and was happy to see me – smiled and reached out her hand. My heart lurched of course.

It was with great relief that I let David know the new medication had been dropped:

Margaret is much better since the morning medication was dropped. This afternoon she wanted to go out (she goes and sits in the car) and I suggested an outing for her benefit to Ken. While he was getting ready I put my arm around her and said, 'We're going to the pharmacy then to Mitchel's farm for vegetables and afterwards we're going to the pub to dance on the tables'. Poker-face she said, 'That's dreadful' – as a punchline.

Tonight she suddenly felt unwell in the middle of dinner. She went and lay down and I went to sit with her. I said, 'How are you feeling, Margie?' She just opened her eyes and looked at me and said, 'Not like an alive person.' As I keep saying, she knows . . .

David had been my sounding board throughout, and the person who really understood what this journey had been like for me. For many years he was long-winded in letters when someone else was typing them for him; now his missives were concise and went straight to the heart of the matter. They kept me sane, they made me laugh at times and they also comforted me enormously. I told him so:

I just want to say that a very strange thing has happened. Because we now communicate via email – not that different from old-fashioned letters – I have fallen in love with you all over again. It's such a strange thing – the way you wrote letters to people used to drive me demented because you were so verbose and repetitive. But learning to type and communicate via email has fined down your writing and I have, in a strange way, rediscovered you. The 'spare' you. The 'say it only once' you. The clever, funny, witty you that has always been there (and that I love) but that has been buried by the anxious you. Communication via writing is a powerful tool which is why people fall in love over the internet (say no more). But for me, it's been a lesson in rediscovering an old love and it makes me very happy.

A few years ago I read a very moving article in the *New Yorker* magazine, written by an elderly man who had just lost the love of his life, his wife of fifty-four years. He was lamenting that he had nothing tangible from her; no letters or even notes that spoke of how much she loved him or how wonderful their relationship had been. They had been side by side for all their lives and there had never been a need for letters to be exchanged. Unlike couples separated by work or war, where heartfelt greetings and words of love travel back and forth, this couple had never written to each other at all. Not once. And now he was distraught that there was nothing he could hold in his hands, nothing to read and read again, to comfort him in his time of grief.

This article stayed with me, and I thought of it while David and I were writing to each other every day, week after week, month after month. I realised that our letters were a valuable part of the healing process in our relationship. That reading his thoughts, expressed so simply, had made me feel closer to him once again. I can't explain it any more clearly. I saw aspects of him I hadn't noticed before. I appreciated his constancy and devotion, against the odds.

The internet has certainly changed the way we all communicate. There is an immediacy about it – you can respond instantly and know what the other person is thinking and feeling. For me, David's letters were a lifeline during this troubling period, and when I got home I intended to print them out and treasure them always.

On the day I turned fifty, I was living in a small French village, revelling in the life of a single woman with a gang of new friends and a stimulating social life. I had been exploring the glorious countryside, discovering fascinating new villages almost every day, acquainting myself with the joys of shopping for food in the local markets, and generally indulging myself in a carefree, self-focused lifestyle.

To celebrate my birthday, I was taken out to a five-course lunch in a rustic village restaurant, then spent the afternoon partying in my friend Jock's courtyard, breaking open several magnums of French champagne and generally behaving in an outrageous fashion.

My fifty-eighth birthday found me in an equally beautiful part of the world, but my sense of recklessness and irresponsibility had long since departed. It had been a busy and rather chaotic morning at my sister's farm, with workmen arriving unexpectedly and disrupting our demanding routine, so I was feeling more than a little frazzled by the time I managed to coax Margaret from her warm bed and wrangle her into a deep, hot bath for a relaxing soak.

I was gently massaging her legs under the water as she floated dreamily, lost in her own world, when I remembered.

'Guess what, Margaret? It's my birthday today.'

Her face instantly changed. She opened her large, pale green eyes and looked up at me with her beautiful smile. She wanted to say something, but was struggling to find the words.

'Well, Merry Christmas to you,' she beamed.

Ken believed that Margaret should be encouraged to continue with as many of her old routines as possible. He still took her shopping at the supermarket and, although she sometimes seemed overwhelmed by the large numbers of people and all the activity, on the whole I thought she still enjoyed these outings. She would push the trolley while we did the run of the aisles as quickly and efficiently as possible. A strange thing had occurred as part of her illness – she had developed a sweet tooth. It's not uncommon, according to the specialist. All her life Margaret had avoided overeating sweets and desserts, yet now she craved them and in the supermarket her eyes lit up at the sight of the cakes and biscuits and tarts.

Indeed Margaret's appetite had increased to the point where she was gaining weight and many of her clothes had started to become very tight around the middle. She was by no means fat – still a small size 12 – but I had to start moving buttons and slipping some extra elastic into waistbands so that her clothes would still fit.

Margaret could no longer dress or undress herself and her arms and hands became uncoordinated and very stiff and awkward. Getting clothes onto her could be very complicated and when I found myself doing this alone I invariably got into a terrible tangle of arms and legs. She looked exasperated and I was generally covered with sweat by the time I got her dressed in the morning. Fedema and Margaret's part-time day carer, Bev, had much more success and I started leaving it to them whenever I could.

Fedema or I took Margaret for a walk at least twice a day. Until recently she used to stride out confidently, but now she tended to shuffle along slowly, as though her feet were no longer connected to the rest of her body. She was often reluctant to go, but once we were out of the front gates she became a little more motivated. I linked arms and sang to her as we walked along, songs I knew she would remember from childhood. Songs I knew my mother would have sung to her as she later sang them to me when I was growing up. There was no doubt Margaret connected with the lyrics and tunes, no matter how bad my rendition. She seemed particularly taken with the songs of Paul Robeson that I knew by heart from an old family record album. She didn't sing along, but she smiled as we wandered in our lurching fashion past farms and woodland.

Last thing at night, after dinner and a wash, once she was dressed in her pyjamas, I sat with Margaret as she settled into bed. I massaged moisturisers into her face and she obviously loved this little bit of pampering. What we all wanted was for Margaret to feel safe and well loved. This next part of her life must be comfortable and trouble-free.

Leaving Margaret and Ken had become increasingly heart-wrenching, but I knew that I needed to get back to the family and finish various work projects that had been temporarily put on the back-burner. I also believed that Fedema must be allowed to manage on her own for a while, to gain her confidence and put her own stamp on this job she has embraced so enthusiastically. Back in the Philippines, Fedema's mother was caring for her children while her husband worked every day in a factory. Here in Canada, Fedema was caring for my sister and holding it all together until I had a chance to come back.

I still found the whole concept sad and difficult.

29

This long journey back from Canada to Australia was my seventh over the last three years. I sometimes feel as though I'm on a merry-go-round, jumping from one continent to the next. Every time I return home there's a period of adjustment – whether it's my home at the farm with David, my home in the village in France, or my sister's home in Canada. I have to get my head around everything all over again and settle myself in. Depending on how long I've been away, I sometimes forget where things are kept or how to use basic appliances or gadgets. I rummage through drawers and cupboards trying to find where things have been stashed in my absence. And I face the continuing challenge of having to adjust to driving on a different side of the road. Right-hand drive in France, left-hand in Australia, then back to the right when I am in Canada. I also leave clothes in all three places, which can cause problems. I have often spent half an hour looking for a particular pair of shoes to go with an outfit, only to remember that I left them in the bottom of the cupboard in France. So I spend a lot of my life reorientating.

I also have to adjust to being with David again, sometimes after separations of three months or more. The initial reunion is always exciting for us both. We fall into each other's arms and, if he's picked me up from the airport in Sydney, we talk non-stop all the way back to the farm. There's so much to catch up on, from family news to quite mundane information. How much water is in the house tank? Have the chickens been laying? How bad are the snakes this summer?

After a few days, we inevitably go through a difficult patch. David has been running the place in my absence and he finds it hard to relinquish control when I return. I am accustomed to organising the domestic side of our lives, especially in the kitchen, which I regard as my domain. Conflict arises when I put things back the way I like them or change anything in the routine he has established in my absence. It becomes a bit of a power struggle, but eventually we manage to work it out. It seems hilarious that at this stage of our lives, after thirty-seven years of being together, we are nitpicking about what should go into the compost bin or whether the eggs should be kept in or out of the fridge. It's the nature of long-term relationships, this constant renegotiation, and I try to laugh about it rather than get cranky.

Often when at home, I have intensive writing to complete and I escape to a motel for a week or ten days so I can concentrate on nothing but getting on top of the task. The first time I did this, during the writing of *Last Tango in Toulouse*, I didn't tell David. I knew I needed solitude, some quiet writing time without interruption, so I waited for him to go to the gym then packed my computer in the truck and drove to the Big Trout Motor Inn at Oberon, where I bunkered down for eight days. He's now accustomed to this eccentricity of mine, running away to write. If I'm working on a section of a book that requires complete focus, I simply can't stay at home because of all the distractions. The meals, the garden, the animals. They pull me away from the essential task at hand. In a motel I have an easy routine. I get up very early and start writing while still in my nightie, drinking tea and eating toast. I don't stop until late afternoon when I go for a walk, have a bite to eat at the local pub, followed by an early night. It's amazing how much writing I can get done in just a few days, and once I gain momentum it's easy to keep it going, even when I get back to the farm.

Over time my grandchildren have also grown accustomed to my comings and goings. When Miriam's older boys were little I was at home most of the time and saw them on a regular basis. Indeed, when the family lived in Bathurst I would see them virtually every day. I would often pick them up from school and bring them out for a swim in the wading pool and afternoon tea. I really missed this when the family moved to Adelaide, so I fly down there as often as possible, and I also try to plan my year so that for at least one of the school holidays I'm at the farm and we fly them up for a week or more. I enjoy these extended visits, even though these days I find keeping up with four lively boys can be exhausting.

I used to see a lot of Isabella and Caius when they lived with us at the farm for two years, even though I was travelling so much. This constant contact has created a deep bond which survives the fact that I'm not around as much these days. Isabella spends a lot of time in hospital so I organise for Caius to stay overnight as often as possible. He calls these visits 'sleepovers' and absolutely adores being an only child for a day or two. I make him special meals, we go for long walks and he loves to help in the vegetable garden and with the poultry. At night he sleeps on a single mattress on the floor of our bedroom. The house is large with long hallways and lots of empty bedrooms, and he's not quite ready to brave one of the spare bedrooms alone.

Hamish and Ella often come over from Mudgee when I'm at the farm, and sometimes I have them for part of the school holidays. If their cousins are also staying I can have up to seven children living-in at a time, and this requires super organisation and a cool head. I am quite strict about certain things, and they totally accept the 'rules' at the farm. No computer or console games; no lolling around in front of the

TV; no eating in front of the TV . . . in fact they are only allowed to eat at the table unless we are having a picnic or sitting out on one of the verandahs. They have to help setting the table and clearing up after a meal and I encourage the older ones to get involved with the cooking, too. Eamonn makes a delicious meatloaf and Sam likes decorating the pavlovas. They eat mountains of food – literally a fridge-full every day – and David is constantly alarmed at how many trips he makes to the supermarket when the kids are staying. One full trolley a day is not uncommon.

I also insist that they all have a 'quiet time' after lunch. They lie down on a bed and read for an hour – I spread them around all the different rooms, because having two in together means there's no reading, just hijinks.

Once again, I'm sad Isabella doesn't often get a chance to be part of these wild and woolly family gatherings. I would not be capable of caring for her and looking after a gang of children at the same time. She only comes to stay overnight if her parents are also staying. I have looked after her on my own quite a few times, and I've even mastered the intricacies of operating her feeding pump and managing her complicated medication. However, now that her epilepsy has intensified she requires constant monitoring and, quite frankly, I don't spend enough time with her to immediately recognise the signs that she could be having a problem. The farm is quite a distance from the nearest hospital and this also makes me nervous.

I've stayed at the house at Blackheath overnight to babysit both children so that Ethan and Lynne can have a night out alone, or with friends. Lynne's parents have also helped tremendously, having the children to stay. But the only time Lynne and Ethan experience total respite from caring is when they have a week at a special care centre for disabled children at the beach in Manly. It's a fantastic concept. The children in need of care are housed upstairs and even a child with disabilities as profound as Isabella's can be looked after twenty-four hours a day. The families are housed in apartments downstairs, only a short walk from the beach. So Lynne, Ethan and Caius have a restful holiday in a beautiful location and they can come and go and spend time with Isabella as often as they please. This suits them so much better than simply leaving Isabella alone in a respite home for a week. They are entitled to support such as this but would much prefer to be as close to her as possible.

As my oldest grandson heads into his teens I suddenly begin to contemplate the next possible stage. Great-grandmotherhood. It may well come to pass, and that's a seriously alarming thought.

30

I couldn't believe I was at the airport again. It's just as well I was such an easy traveller, because my life at that time was spent hanging around airport lounges and dashing to make connecting flights . . .

I don't travel business class because I find it a huge cost to pay for a day in your life spent in the air. But I have developed a few techniques of my own for making it bearable. A glass of wine at the airport, of course, and I always treat myself to a new book to read along the way. I go for an aisle seat and carry a cashmere shawl to wrap myself in – as well as the blanket that's provided. I can't sleep if I'm cold. I eat the meal provided, with a glass of wine, and take a sleeping pill. With luck I'll sleep six to seven hours straight, then when I wake I'll watch movies or read until we arrive. It's almost as if I put myself into hibernation mode for the period of time it takes me to get from A to B.

Travelling from the farm near Bathurst to my house in France can take more than thirty-five hours door to door, depending on the connections. David drops me at the little airport near town, and the flight to Sydney takes forty minutes at most. I then catch the underground train to the international airport and check in, always allowing plenty of time. The flight from Sydney to London takes around twenty-four hours, with one stop along the way. I transfer to another terminal and catch a flight to Paris, which only takes an hour – it's the waiting around and clearing security that takes so long. After I clear customs I catch a taxi across the city – always wide-eyed with delight to be back in France – to Gare d'Austerlitz, where I board a train for the five-hour journey south to the elegant town of Gourdon. At the Paris railway station there is a restaurant that I just love. It's simple but they always have en excellent *plat* and I order a small bottle of red wine to remind myself that I really am here, at last.

Rail travel in France is fast, and better than most equivalent Australian services. The carriages are comfortable, the trains generally run on time, and the scenery speeding past the window is entrancing. Much to my amusement, passengers are allowed to bring their animals into the carriages. Once, I sat next to a woman with a poodle on her lap. Another time, I was caught up in a nasty dogfight. While everyone was asleep, two dogs – one large mutt and a small lapdog – took advantage of the situation to attack each other. By the time their owners woke there was blood all over the carriage and both dogs looked worse for wear.

This trip, I find myself opposite a young couple with a ferret in a cage – urgh! – and I am bemused by its antics. It tries to escape, savagely attacking the bars with its sharp little teeth. Then it sleeps deeply for an hour, on its back with its feet in the air. Then it piddles on the towel lining its cage. The acrid smell of rodent-like urine fills the carriage, but the young couple sleep on, oblivious to the fact that their pet is stinking us out.

In Gourdon I am met by a friend – sometimes Jock, sometimes another member of my gang – and then it's a thirty-five-minute drive to the house in Frayssinet. It's such a joy to arrive.

This time, I was here to lead one of my tours and there was a lot to be done as it was a big group – nineteen people, including a woman from New York who found our details on the internet – and, at eighteen days, quite a long tour. I had allowed myself a fortnight to unwind before starting work in earnest.

The next day I did as I always do when I arrive in France. I joined a group of friends for lunch at Restaurant Murat in the nearby tiny village of Pomarede. The restaurant is now regularly invaded by groups of travelling Australians who have read the book I wrote about it several years ago. A copy is proudly displayed on the bar, and Mme Murat – Jeannette – and her daughter Sylvie are delighted that the restaurant's fame has spread so far. Five generations of women have owned and operated this working man's restaurant for more than one hundred years, and they serve the traditional, family-cooked meals of the region. Sylvie has officially taken over the day-to-day running of the establishment, although her mother still lives upstairs in the rooms where she was born and where her father and grandmother also entered the world. Jeannette remains a constant presence, fussing over people as they arrive, taking orders and clearing the tables. Having lunch here is always a delight, although it can be a struggle getting up from the table after five courses and all that red wine.

Some friends had been lent a house for a week on the Atlantic coast, in a charming resort town called Hossegor. It's north of Biarritz, the famous surfing mecca, and only an hour from the Spanish border. Usually when I'm in the south-west of France I'm inclined to hang around the region where we have the house rather than explore too much further afield. It's partly laziness, because I just love sinking into village life and becoming part of the local scene again, but it's also financial. Why would I want to pay for hotel rooms when I have a lovely house of my own?

My friends were already at the beach house when I arrived in France, and I decided to drive over for just a few days. It would be about a three-hour journey. My car is very old and lacks modern comforts such as air conditioning or a GPS for directions, however, I found a website with detailed directions on driving across country and I set off optimistically, with my instructions printed out in large handwriting on a piece of paper on the passenger seat. I find this is the easiest method when driving alone, because I can stop quickly to check on the next town I should be heading for without having to change into reading glasses and look at the fine print on a map.

Somehow I got totally tangled up in the town of Agen, and ended up travelling south instead of south-west, running through all sorts of little villages and settlements that are completely off the beaten track. I was determined not to get flustered by this, but to just enjoy the drive. Eventually I would find my way to the coast.

The day turned out to be very hot indeed. Sweat was pouring down my face, and I seemed to be driving around in circles. I was sure there were several villages I had been through more than once. I arrived in a large, elegant town with glorious old buildings set around a winding canal, and on checking my position realised I was in Condom. Local Brits laugh about the name of this place and now I was smack bang in the middle of it, quite accidentally. I continued on, repeating the mantra that I should just enjoy the ride, but the novelty was rapidly wearing off. Thank heavens I had my mobile phone with me and managed to get through to my friends, who gave me some quick directions on how to reach them. They worked! Almost six hours after leaving Frayssinet I arrived in Hossegor, looking forward to a cool drink and a swim in the ocean.

This region of France is famous for its fresh seafood, and we decided to eat nothing but that for the entire short holiday. We went to the morning markets on the wharf and bought crabs and all sorts of fresh fish to barbeque for our evening meal. My friends are real foodies and we literally stuffed ourselves with delicious food, day after day. One day we decided to drive across the border into Spain for lunch. I'd never been into Spain and the thought of cruising the tapas bars was most appealing. It all sounds very extravagant, but in fact it's not an enormously expensive day out. It would cost more to have lunch in a reasonably good restaurant in Sydney or Melbourne. I was struck by how different Spain is from France. It's that old border thing – the moment you cross over into Spain the atmosphere changes immediately. The tapas bars were great fun and the food was fantastic. Not too heavy, but with lots of seafood and intense flavours. We swam in the ocean again and I slept really well that night! I felt rested, as though I'd had a proper break.

Back in Frayssinet, I began to get organised for the tour with the help of my friend Jan, who lives full time in France and acts as our local guide. We try to incorporate a little bit of everything into these trips: history, architecture, scenery, farm life, local culture, fresh air, exercise and, of course, great food and wine. Having conducted five of these tours, I've discovered the most memorable aspect for many tourists is the opportunity to meet locals and go into their homes – even if it's just for a drink or a coffee. It's the sort of thing most people don't get to experience when they're travelling.

From my perspective, I get a kick out of meeting a diverse group of people from all over Australia who have one common passion: they love France and they're keen to explore this relatively remote area, embracing all it has to offer. A bond develops as we get into the journey, and I'm also intrigued by how people on group tours link up, forming unexpected alliances. Given that their paths may never cross back home in Australia, new friendships are forged and I enjoy that notion of bringing people together in a shared adventure.

This time we had a lot of husbands along for the ride, which gave gender balance to the group. In the past we have had maybe ten or twelve women and just a couple of blokes, but for once we had six husbands and wives, a couple of single women and some women also travelling in pairs. With more 'attached' men, the group dynamic changes. Women travelling alone tend to be more raucous and uninhibited; having the blokes around has a slightly sobering effect.

But there's always at least one comedian in a group, someone with quick one-liners or a seemingly endless stream of bad jokes to tell on the bus. This year there were a couple, including a delightful chap who suffered from a touch of 'some mothers do 'ave 'em' syndrome. He seemed accident-prone and was always bumping or knocking or dropping something – usually a large glass of red wine and usually all over himself. It became a real running gag, waiting for his daily disaster, and even our bus driver was amused by his antics.

One of the highlights of this tour was having lunch in the garden of my friends Trish Hobbs and Dany Chouet, who live in an ancient stone house with a beautiful garden near Monpazier, one of the unusual planned and fortified towns from medieval times – *bastides*, the French call them – which can be found in this region. For decades Dany and Trish owned Cleopatra, the famous country guesthouse and restaurant at Blackheath in the Blue Mountains, and although they have retired to France they were delighted to welcome our lively group for a picnic lunch in their garden. It was a perfect day and the food was very special – homemade tomato flans and succulent rolled loin of pork with salads, followed by various local cheeses and fruit tarts for dessert. We lingered so long in the garden, sipping wine, that we had to skip the *château* we were intending to visit after lunch.

Another highlight was meeting the Australian artist Erica de Jong, who lives with her husband Henk in the celebrated artists' colony Saint-Cirq Lapopie. Erica and Henk have been restoring ruined cottages to rent out as holiday houses and their creativity in these renovations was inspiring. They invited the group to look over their own small house, perched high on a cliff edge overlooking the Lot river, and many people commented afterwards that it was the most spectacular slice of France they had ever seen.

The final leg of this trip was to the historic city of Albi, famous as the birthplace of Toulouse-Lautrec. We hadn't included this on the itinerary before and it turned out to be very special – in particular being given a guided tour of the *château* where he was born.

On our last day we had lunch together in Toulouse, taking over the front of one of the pretty little cafes in the square, and as usual at least one glass of wine was knocked over.

31

After the French tour I had only a couple of days to unwind, and then packed up the house to head for Canada again. I hated packing up – stripping the beds and closing the shutters – especially as I had no idea when I would return to my beloved cottage. I had a few tenants coming and that helped, knowing that the house would be inhabited and not sitting cold and lonely all through the long winter. I yearned for those long visits I used to have, where I stayed for four or five months at a time, writing and sitting far too long in the sun drinking wine with my friends. They seem like a carefree, distant past to me now that my life involves so much trans-Atlantic travel. I don't regret for a moment my decision to do this, but sometimes I hanker for that lovely sense of freedom I had when I first escaped to France. I am sure there are many others in my situation, probably caring for aged parents, and feeling a little trapped again – just as they did during the years when their children were growing up.

Every time I leave Canada I find it hard to imagine how Margaret's condition could be any worse, yet every time I return I am shocked at her ongoing decline. I shouldn't be shocked because I am always forewarned, either by Ken during our phone calls, or by Fran via emails. Unless you are there witnessing it, it's really difficult to visualise the progress of this disease, so when I leave I hold a picture in my mind of Margaret and when I return that Margaret has vanished and a new one has appeared.

The first thing I noticed, the morning after my late flight in from London, was that Margaret's anxiety had almost disappeared, which was a relief in some ways. She had lost that haunted and confused face – it had been replaced by a blank visage. She could still make eye contact and respond with a smile, even an occasional word, but for much of the time she was lost in her own world, staring vacantly into space. It was something Ken and I feared and finally here it was. She had lost the spirit to fight against the routine intervention that punctuated her life. Where once she would resist getting up in the morning, she now went along with it willingly, although her ability to do so had greatly decreased. She virtually had to be lifted in and out of the bathtub, and her arms and legs found it hard to cooperate when it came to dressing.

This new stage meant that Margaret could sit calmly and no longer paced frantically looking for something to do. She didn't move things around as often (where did my pillows go? I found them later in the freezer) and she didn't try to leave the house, mainly because she could no longer manage even a single downward step unaided and there are steps into and out of every entrance.

Margaret could barely put one foot in front of another when we wheedled her out of bed in the morning. Once she got going she could walk unassisted, but still very gingerly. She looked as though she was walking on eggshells. She no longer had spatial concepts so she couldn't judge where she was putting her feet or where she needed to position herself to sit down. She had to be guided in all these things. Indeed she needed assistance with every aspect of her everyday life. Waking, sleeping, standing, sitting, eating, drinking and going to the toilet.

She would lose her balance and needed to be supervised all the time. Four weeks before I arrived she fell in the night and broke her arm. She didn't tell anyone about her injury and it was only discovered the following morning when Fedema went to get her up and saw her twisted, swollen wrist. The second night I was there Margaret fell out of bed yet again, and Ken, fast asleep, didn't realise for some time. He called out urgently for help; even though the house is centrally heated she felt quite cold by the time Fedema and I placed her back beneath the warm covers.

I wondered about Margaret's perception of pain. Why didn't she call for help when she broke her arm? Probrobly she was incapable of a normal response – not realising she should be calling out for help. It was very frightening. Fedema watched my sister like a hawk and I had to learn to be as vigilant when she was in my care. The most positive thing, from my perspective, was that Fedema had bonded with both Margaret and Ken, and had made a huge difference to their quality of life. She and Margaret now had a tender relationship and she managed the daily routine of waking, bathing, feeding and medication so well that Margaret remained calm and unflustered. Fedema was warm and affectionate, often sitting for an hour looking at books with Margaret and linking arms to take her for long walks so that Ken could rest and have a break. Margaret's clothes were immaculate, her nails were trimmed and her skin was glowing because Fedema massaged creams into her legs, arms and face after every morning bath. She could not be better cared for.

Fedema wanted to vist her relatives in Vancouver, and had organised to take some time off while I was around. I thought it was a great idea because I worried that she would burn out with the constant demands of caring for Margaret.

In the few years since our reunion, Margaret has gradually lost her language skills. She no longer had the ability to find the right words and so she lived in a cone of silence. Sometimes, very occasionally, she attempted a conversation, but it was heart-wrenching to watch her floundering, gesticulating with her hands to express what she was desperately trying to convey. Sometimes, I could pick up a sense of what she was telling me – word associations provided hints and clues that helped me, in turn, to find the right words to respond. But just as often the words came out in a jumble – some words were not words at all but some strange dialect – so that all I could do was nod and agree.

Every so often, but increasingly less frequently, Margaret would come out with a totally lucid sentence or an expression completely appropriate to the situation or the discussion that was going on around her. These were the cruellest moments of all, because it's then we were reminded that Margaret is still in there somewhere, trapped inside her damaged mind and still capable of knowing and feeling. It's easy to fall into the trap of believing that a person in the last stages of dementia is a mental vegetable. That they are incapable of any comprehension or reason. Childlike and mentally defective. They certainly are not.

David was the recipient of my darkest thoughts, and I used my emails to him to record some of my gloomiest moments.

Margaret has been up and down. I have been bringing her into my room for an afternoon nap (to give Ken a break) and now she wants to sleep in here all the time which is not a good idea (from my perspective – also from Ken's) so I had to wrangle her into her own bed and stroke her off to sleep. I can say it's easier looking after all eight of our grandchildren at once (including Isabella) than caring for Marge. It's the greatest tug of love I have ever known. More tomorrow.

She has no concept of space. She can't sit down on a chair without being backed up and lowered down. She can't stand without being helped up. Getting in and out of the car takes fifteen minutes. When we walk she pulls to the left – one side of her brain isn't working – so she would end up in a ditch if I wasn't constantly pulling her back onto the path.

Sometimes she just rests her head on my shoulder and sighs. It's awful – beyond awful.

I cannot begin to tell you how tragic this all is. Please don't worry so much, darling. It's just that when things happen that move me deeply I have nobody to tell but you. Every day is a bit different and for me the knowledge that deep inside Margaret knows what's going on makes it so much worse. There's nothing she can do about it – just live it. Just imagine if you had forgotten everything and felt lost all the time – that's how it is.

But I also tell him the bright and funny things that somehow help make the whole difficult time more bearable.

Tonight we had dinner at Fran's which was lovely, but difficult as usual. She'd made pasta, which Margaret wasn't managing very well. At one point Fran asked her, 'How do you like the pasta, Marge?' 'B minus,' was the reply. We fell off our chairs laughing. Old teachers never die . . .

Laughter is of paramount importance for family and carers dealing with Alzheimer's. It's not that we laugh at Margaret herself, because we don't. We know she would laugh just as heartily if she could stand back and see some of the situations, although I know she would also be appalled to find herself in this condition. We laugh because it breaks the tension and allows us to share the sadness in a lighter vein, just for a moment. We all have to go on living and have some brightness in our lives even though Margaret's life and grasp on the world is shrinking, shrivelling before our eyes.

Apart from being a wonderfully warm teacher, a highly qualified academic and a champion of art education in Canada, my sister Margaret was also a fine artist. I grew up with just one painting in our house that she left behind when she fled the family all those years ago. It's a street scene in Darlinghurst, Sydney, just near East Sydney Tech where she studied art before completing her Dip. Ed. to become an art teacher. This charming work now hangs in her brother Jon's house in Warialda.

On one of my visits to Vancouver Island, Ken took me down into the basement to show me a timber framework that Margaret had built to store her unmounted artworks, and I was astonished at the tremendous variety of styles and materials that she had used over the years. There were oils and acrylics and watercolours, charcoals and line drawings and woodcuts, calligraphy and collages and lots of experimental works. Some paintings were very dark and dramatic; some light and full of movement and colour. She painted scenes and people and villages in France and Italy and old buildings in the UK and rustic farm scenes, including sketches of Ken at work in their garden.

I was enchanted by the images she had produced, but by this stage Margaret had lost interest in her art. She had stopped painting and her studio was a riot of disorder. The floor was covered with boxes and bags and the desk was thirty centimetres deep in artworks gathering dust. It was a pathetic reflection of how disordered her mind had been as her condition had gradually deteriorated. She had spent so many happy hours in this studio, working away on her various creative projects. And now it was a muddle.

Every Wednesday is art group day, and even though Margaret no longer paints, Ken takes her to the lunch each week as an outing and to keep her in touch with her former life. This time Ken suggested we should host the art group at their place and I thought it was a great idea, although Margaret would probably retreat during the painting and talking part of the proceedings and emerge only at lunchtime.

I made soup and we contributed a roasted chicken. The other women brought all sorts of savoury dishes, salads, meats and platters of fruit along with cakes and slices. In the past I have made pavlovas for these gatherings, and it always ends up being a debate about whether the recipe is Australian or originally from New Zealand. One of the group is a New Zealander, needless to say, and she and I have also disagreed about the origin of pikelets. It's highly entertaining.

I told the group of my dilemma over Margaret's artwork. I was concerned that even though the basement and studio were dry, the paintings would deteriorate badly if just left the way they were. I needed advice on the best way to conserve this precious aspect of my sister's life. The group sprang to life with offers of help and suggestions about ways of protecting the paintings: folders and portfolios and special paper that preserves the paint and dustproof boxes. They also suggested we make contact with a former colleague of Margaret's who still had a connection with the university where she taught, who might know of a way the paintings could be preserved as a collection.

Ken called Margaret's old workmate, who immediately expressed interest in the idea. He decided to come out the following weekend to look through the paintings and give us an opinion. I was spurred into action. I looked at the studio and quite honestly couldn't think where to start. I wanted to restore a sense of order and harmony, but I didn't want to strip it bare, to take away Margaret's imprint.

I started sorting through the artworks, putting them into piles according to the style and the material used. I felt a bit strange invading my sister's private space, yet again, although this time it was like rifling through a wonderful treasure trove. There were some exquisite miniatures and a collection of ink drawings of cats which had been done for a children's book that was never published. I just loved them.

As I dug through the layers of precious works mixed up with debris I found some astonishing things. For decades, Margaret and Ken made Christmas stockings for all the members of the family, and I found plastic bags stuffed with all sorts of treats intended for the stockings – she obviously bought them, hid them in the studio, then completely forgot about them. The dockets, still in the plastic bags, dated back four years, which must have been a critical time for her memory loss. Just as I found in her bedroom drawers, there were unpaid bills and uncashed cheques and unfinished letters and photographs all jumbled together. Most of her more recent artworks were unfinished.

It took me three days to restore order. The bookshelves, groaning with volumes of art history, were dusted. I found a copy of her PhD thesis and examples of various educational programs she designed while working at the university. It was like looking down a long corridor into her past life; that huge part of her life when I didn't know her and she had no knowledge of me. There were pieces of art I loved so much I just wanted to frame them and take them home, and Ken kept suggesting I should take whatever I liked. But I couldn't bring myself to take a single thing. I felt uncomfortable with the thought of removing anything from her studio while she was still here, wandering in and out from time to time. To me, it was still very much her special place, as though she might one day walk in again, sit down and pick up a paintbrush.

On the weekend we were visited by Margaret's old friend, who greeted her tenderly; she smiled broadly in return, and for a moment there was a flicker of recognition. I showed him the works I had sorted in the studio and also the ones I had carefully wrapped in the basement. He was most impressed by her body of work – I suspected her fellow academics didn't realise she had such an active life as an artist outside her day job as an assistant professor.

Her friend suggested that a selection of Margaret's works should be included in a large exhibition at the university gallery the following year. He believed it would be appropriate to make a special feature of Margaret, as the exhibition was to celebrate the anniversary of the art education department where she worked for so long. There would be a catalogue and a tribute in it to her, which I could help to write. I was thrilled. Ken was thrilled. In such a short time our problem about caring for her works had been solved and the bonus was that Margaret would be recognised for the talented and dedicated woman that she had always been.

32

It had been nearly three months since I was at home and David and I had an urgent need to spend some time together after what had been a hectic and, at times, harrowing year. In among our heartfelt exchanges about Margaret's condition, more personal and loving emails were flying back and forth, a reflection of the strength of our new relationship. David even started doing something I would never have thought imaginable for him – sending me sexy emails about his plans for my return. He'd stocked the pantry and cellar with good food and wine and he was proposing we lock ourselves up at the farm for a few days and just have fun. This was so unlike the old David; the work-driven, self-absorbed David. He'd become so much more communicative and romantic that I almost wondered if he was drawing on some film script for inspiration. But I wasn't about to quibble. I was thrilled by his enticing words and it made me hunger to jump on the plane and head home to be with him.

This desire was counterbalanced by the knowledge that in leaving I also had to say goodbye again to Margaret and Ken. I wasn't worried about them in any immediate sense as I knew they were now very well cared for and that their physical health was not fragile as such. It was just that I had an appreciation of how much moral support I was able to offer them during what was easily the most difficult time of their lives. I knew how Ken's spirits lifted when I was there to spend time talking to him and listening to his poignant reminiscences of his life with Margaret. I also knew that Margaret became more animated and lively when I was around. Just having one extra pair of hands to help made a tremendous difference.

We had a lovely last evening meal together and then for the first time Margaret didn't come to say goodbye at the airport because it was a night flight and she was already tucked into bed. I said goodnight, and gave her my usual gentle face massage as she drifted off, and I reminded her that I was leaving and wouldn't see her again for some time. She didn't seem to register this information at all.

I hugged Ken and promised to return as soon as I could, and dashed for the little plane to Vancouver city. The long, tedious flight home allowed me plenty of time for reflection and I thought constantly about Margaret and the quality of her life as it was at that moment, and then into the future.

I am aware that a decade ago I would have been a keen advocate for euthanasia for anyone in Margaret's situation. When you view people's circumstances from a distance, using intellect rather than heart and emotion to make judgements, then mercy killing of people with advanced dementia may seem an acceptable, even desirable, option. But from where I now stand, up close and totally involved, the thought of 'putting her out of her misery' is abhorrent to me.

There are many levels to this argument. I feel strongly that if Margaret were in any position to make the decision for herself then she would undoubtedly opt not to continue with her life. Margaret has always been an intensely private, self-sufficient and independent woman. She has carried with her the scars of her sad childhood and teenage years and risen above all these obstacles to create a happy and fulfilling life for herself. She has enjoyed a successful career and marriage and she lives in a beautiful home environment that is very much of her own making. She has a wide circle of good friends and a small circle of very dear friends; she has always fostered warm relationships with Ken's family and she has enjoyed travelling and music and art and literature. She can't participate in any of these things any more. She has been reduced to a shell of her former self. A frail and addled person who can only muddle through each day with a great deal of physical assistance and support and love from those around her.

That's the crux of it: love. Margaret is still very much a loved and valued member of her family, and I am quite certain she still feels emotions such as love as well. It's obvious to me that she feels frustration and confusion and even anger at times because she has enough awareness to know that something completely out of her control has taken over her body and her life. Yet when she smiles, or reaches out a hand, or puts her head on a shoulder, or gives a spontaneous hug, there's no doubt that the loving Margaret still exists inside that shell.

There are all the legal and ethical questions, of course. Who makes that decision about 'if and when' another person should die? Margaret is certainly in no state of mind to make any decisions at all, let alone life-and-death decisions. Do the husband or wife or children decide? Do the doctors decide? Does a panel that includes family and members of the medical profession decide? I would have to say no to all of these options. It's just not a decision anyone can make for anyone else, regardless of the situation.

I'm not anti-euthanasia per se, but many aspects of its implementation disturb me deeply, and I think we are a long way from working through all the legal and ethical arguments to create a model that works perfectly in our society. Certainly I oppose it in situations such as Margaret's, where she has lost cognitive function to the point where she's incapable of deciding the time is right to die. Certainly I'm against it in situations such as my grand-daughter Isabella's, where she has mental and physical disabilities that have made her childhood such a difficult and at times painful journey. She's a child, and cannot make such a decision for herself, therefore nobody has a right to make that decision on her behalf.

There's another feeling that never leaves me. In these sad situations, the people around the sufferer – the family and the friends and the close carers – have an opportunity to express their love and devotion in many wonderful ways. Looking after Margaret can be soul-destroying and exhausting and frustrating and heartbreaking. Yet, equally, it is often uplifting and heart-warming and tender and satisfying. When I sit on the edge of her bath massaging her arms and legs with soothing oils, I know I am giving of myself to her and making the quality of her life as good as it possibly can be under these distressing circumstances. I have learned a lot about myself through this experience. I have learned that I can be patient and slow-moving, which are not my usual qualities. I've always charged at life like a bull at a gate. My children were all out of bed, bathed, dressed and breakfasted before they had time to think about it. I'm a speedy person: David calls me hyperactive. Caring for Margaret has taught me to slow down – I simply can't hurry her and so, willingly, I surrender to the beauty of being her carer. Of slowly walking at her side, supporting her all the way, no matter how long the journey or how difficult.

I'm very scared at the prospect of Margaret dying. I'm scared that it will be drawn out and painful and, quite possibly, humiliating and frightening for her. But I don't know what else to do but remain at her side as much as I can right through this whole awful business. I know Ken feels exactly the same way.

I've always believed that birth is a natural process and that we should resist medical intervention as much as humanly possible. The pain and difficulty of birth somehow prepares the parents for the pain and difficulty that must sometimes accompany caring for that child. Death is a bit the same way. It's part of our life journey but, sadly, there is a lot of medical intervention that prolongs life and therefore makes that pain last longer than it should otherwise. We are trapped in this cycle. Without her medication I feel certain Margaret and others in her situation would be 'demented' in the true sense of the word. But perhaps they wouldn't live as long – they would explode in a frenzy of anxiety and confusion and their descent into a coma would be much more rapid.

A coma. That's what we have been told to expect. A point at which Margaret can no longer get out of bed and walk. She will curl up and entirely shut out the rest of the world.

I don't know how I will feel when that day comes.

33

When Margaret and I were reunited in 2002, our most intense conversations revolved around our relationships with our late father, Theo. From my sister's perspective, her problems with him were the motivating force that drove her from our family home and kept her from making contact with us for nearly fifty years. My anger with him was not as intense, but I also disdained his lifestyle and behaviour.

These days, however, I sometimes feel I have judged my father harshly. On the surface it may not appear so. He was indeed a hard-drinking, self-absorbed man who was unfaithful to his wife and had an explosive temper that led to domestic violence. He smoked and gambled and frittered away ever pound he ever earned, leaving his family financially insecure and emotionally drained.

However, as I approach sixty, there are aspects of my father's character that I can finally appreciate. The fact that he killed himself at the age of sixty-two is a telling key to his personality, and one that I think I at last understand.

Dad simply did not want to grow old. He had abused his body with alcohol and tobacco and he looked ravaged. Indeed, looking back at the few family photographs we have of him – like me, he took all the photos and was therefore seldom in them – I can see that from the age of forty he looked much, much older than his years. I have one photo of him in his late fifties, and in it he looks considerably older and more weather-beaten than David does now, even though he is about to turn seventy.

At the first sign of disruptive physical illness – he had a hiatus hernia, not so easy to repair surgically in those days as it is now – my father made the decision that he did not wish to continue living. As I've also described, I believe he suffered from undiagnosed manic depression or bipolar disorder. Combined with the fact that he and my mother were in the midst of a messy and dramatic marriage break-up, these were no doubt the major factors that led to his death. He used alcohol and sleeping pills and didn't leave a note.

Although he grew up in the slums of Melbourne, his mother recognised that her third son was bright and talented, and managed to get him into Melbourne High School, where he attained sufficiently good marks to land a job as a copy boy and then later a cadet journalist on the Melbourne *Herald*. Not bad for a boy from Fitzroy.

Like many outstanding journalists of the era he was proudly 'self-educated', in the sense that he was a voracious reader and acquired a broad general knowledge and a love of literature by burying himself in books. In his early twenties he met and fell in love with the beautiful Veronica, who came from a much more comfortably-off family. Theo wanted to travel and managed to get a job as a steward on an ocean liner bound for London. He no doubt had his eyes on Fleet Street. Veronica joined him after a few months and they hastily married. My half-brother, Jon, was born four months later, so it would seem that Veronica only discovered her pregnancy after Theo had left Australia, and fled the family home to be with him overseas. Needless to say, her parents did not approve of the union.

My father was politicised by the Great Depression, and joined the Communist Party, as many creative and intellectual people did at the time. Unlike most of them, however, he remained a member until the day he died. I have a photograph of him taking part in the massive hunger marches that took place in London in the late twenties and early thirties as unemployed workers from all over Britain converged on the capital to draw attention to their plight. Sometimes, when I was a kid, he used to let me feel the bump on his skull where he'd been bashed by a bobby's truncheon during one of these demonstrations.

He never made it to Fleet Street. After a year in London, the young couple returned to Melbourne where Dad got a job on the *Sun News-Pictorial*. My sister, Margaret, was born during this period. Theo was earning four pounds a week when he was poached by Sir Frank Packer to work as a reporter on the *Daily Telegraph* in Sydney. His new wage was seven pounds, which was quite a princely sum in those days.

It was 1940 when the family moved to Sydney and Sir Frank organised an apartment for them in Double Bay. Life looked rosy but there were problems in the marriage. Later that same year Veronica committed suicide. This devastated our father, and my mother maintained that he never fully recovered from the shock of his young first wife's death. Nobody will ever know the exact circumstances leading up to her tragic decision, but my mother suggested in conversations with me during the years she lived with us at Leura that Theo had been womanising, and carried a huge burden of guilt.

My father was a driven man, but not particularly ambitious. His work promotions came as a result of his natural talent for journalism and his strong work ethic. In spite of his alcoholism, which became chronic during the period when they lived in America, he never missed work or failed to meet a deadline. His articles and columns were spare and beautifully written and he was a stickler for correct grammar and fact checking. I grew up in a house where the news was the most important focus of every day. Every newspaper was read and dissected from the front page to the sports section, and heaven help anybody who spoke or made a noise at seven o'clock when the evening news was broadcast on ABC radio. That half-hour was sacred.

Politics was a constant topic of discussion in our home, and our father inculcated us with his left-wing views and his philosophy of life. He was passionately anti-religion and I was banned from Sunday school, which worried me for many years. I remember begging to be allowed to join a Christian girls' fellowship (the Girls' Friendly Society) and he told me they were a bunch of lesbians. I went to school and said I was not allowed to be a member of the group because they were lesbians, and I couldn't fathom why I was ordered outside to stand in the corridor. A note was sent home and I remember Dad laughing with delight at my naïvety.

He was not an affectionate or demonstrative man but we respected him and, I believe, tried to please him. He wasn't easily able to offer praise, but he was considerate in funny ways. Some of the attitudes he adhered to rigidly have stayed with me all my life. Never be late (I'm always early). Never keep anyone waiting. Always have the correct change. Always offer your seat to others on public transport. Always allow others to go ahead of you in lines or queues. Always wear well-polished shoes (he cleaned our school shoes with spit and polish every Sunday night). Always meet your deadline!

My father could be utterly charming when he wanted to, especially around women. He was greatly admired by many of the men and women he worked with over the years, who had never witnessed his dark side, such as his temper and the violence he directed towards our mother. He never once raised a hand to me, but he did have a couple of wild fistfights with Dan when my brother reached his teens and became disobedient. I suspect it was Dan who threw the first punch.

My father never read to me or held me on his lap, but I loved the way he smelled (aftershave, I guess) and I looked forward to him coming home every night even though I knew it might be another evening of arguments and hostility. I used to hang out of my bedroom window and watch for him walking up from the tram stop at the bottom of the road. He always had a loaf of fresh bread under his arm and a flagon of claret. Dad had a great sense of humour and was very witty and interesting to talk to. He didn't talk to me all that often (his head was always in a book and his hand was always around a glass of red) but when he did I found our conversations thrilling. He made me laugh, he teased me and taught me not to take myself too seriously. He also loved to introduce us to us risqué poems and songs, which used to drive our mother crazy. In the conservative 1950s, Dad was singing us ditties about priests with huge testicles and about Oscar Wilde's sexual proclivities.

He didn't play with us but he took us fishing at Balmoral Beach wharf if we were prepared to get up before dawn to join him. I loved it. We caught leatherjacket and tailor and took them home where Mum would fry them up for breakfast. When I was a teenager he inherited some money after the death of his remarkable mother and he bought a yacht, which he moored in Mosman Bay. We went sailing together – Jon, Dan, Dad and me – and this was the closest I ever felt to him.

Dad was highly respected as a journalist. After the war he rose through the ranks to become the editor of the *Sunday Telegraph*. He wrote book reviews every week, and got the paper out on time in spite of meddling from Sir Frank, who often arrived at the *Telegraph* offices late on Saturday night, drunk and cranky if he had lost money at the races, to try to get our father to change the front-page story. Dad would stand up to him and Sir Frank obviously thought very highly of him, although he had no idea that his editor was a card-carrying member of the Communist Party (Mosman Branch!).

When I joined Australian Consolidated Press as a copy girl in 1968 I was stampeded by people who just wanted to tell me how much they loved and respected my father. From the editor of the *Women's Weekly*, Esme Fenston, down, they considered him to have been the brightest, best and kindest journalist ever to have worked for that organisation (no wonder I had little difficulty getting a job). Even to this day, in the course of my own work, I meet veteran women journalists who remember my dad and have nothing but good things to say about him.

He left the Packer organisation in the 1960s to work as the editor of the Waterside Workers' newspaper for two years while the regular editor was on sabbatical in Moscow (where else?). He took a massive drop in salary to do this job, and no doubt alienated himself permanently from his former employers. For him it was a strong political statement: he was frustrated with the double life he had led for so many years, a dedicated closet leftie who was editor of an ostensibly conservative tabloid newspaper. After this job ended he was editor of the *Mosman Daily*, again on a much lower salary than he had earned in his prime; this was the beginning of his physical and mental decline.

Although I felt a sense of relief when he died because of the terrible pain he was causing our mother, I now admit I loved him dearly despite his selfish and at times irrational ways. That's pretty normal, I guess. I know that Margaret expressed no such tenderness for him at all. Yet Ken has told me that after she heard of Theo's death through a handful of friends in Australia with whom she was still in touch, he found her lying on her bed and crying. It's so very sad.

I look like my dad. I have his wiry red hair, square jaw and pale, freckled skin. I have his smile, his eyes and also his wicked sense of humour. I'm driven to achieve, just as he was, and have also inherited his strong work ethic. I have many of his failings, including being an addictive personality with a penchant for wine and a wild streak sexually that has caused problems in my marriage. I don't have his quick temper and I'm not prone to violence, although I did once punch David very hard during the period when our relationship was floundering. I don't know who was more shocked and horrified – David or me.

I suspect I have inherited some of my father's charm and his ability to work well with others. His talent for writing? It's hard to know because I was brought up with a pen in my hand and writing is as natural to me as walking. We were all big readers, and this inevitably hones writing skills, and Dad was particular about correcting us if we made a mistake – as was our mother – so we certainly had training from a very early age. I'm a stickler for putting commas in the right places, and using the correct form of the superlative.

I see some of my father's strengths and weaknesses in my own children, and I'm aware that it's impossible to avoid his genes, both good and bad. I have reached an age and a stage in my life where I am prepared to admit to myself that I am indeed very much like the man of whom I have been so critical and judgemental in the past. I don't necessarily like this fact, but it's impossible to resile from it.

34

Somewhere, around the age of fifty-one and a half, I lost myself. I simply ceased being me.

Well that's not entirely true. My name remained the same and I still had the same husband, the same four adult children, the same six grandchildren and the same house in the Blue Mountains where I had lived for twenty-five years.

But the me that I had known, and more importantly the me that my family had known for the last thirty years, had transformed into somebody else.

My friends noticed. Many commented. My family looked at me curiously; they were baffled and bemused. The happy-go-lucky, easygoing me became a sharpish, more critical woman. Introspective, self-absorbed and fragile. The woman who had always allowed the rough and tumble of life to wash over her suddenly became hypersensitive, reactive, restless and easily ruffled.

What was going on here? I shed weight, abandoned my straw-hat, rose-pruning image from my days on *Gardening Australia* and morphed into a strawberry blonde in high heels, fishnet tights and figure-hugging clothes. I discarded habits of a lifetime. The world news on the pages of the morning newspaper suddenly seemed unutterably dull, and I rarely read past the headlines. My lifelong passion for reading novels – one or two a week – vanished. I no longer had the concentration required. My love of classical music, instilled from childhood, was replaced by a passion for popular CDs. Plaintive, wailing songs that allowed me to further wallow in self-obsession.

Of course, it's not uncommon for women (and men) to hit a point in their lives when they need to stop and take stock. Need to analyse the past and ponder the future. For men, this stage has traditionally described as the 'midlife crisis', often culminating in the first wife being abandoned for a new, younger partner and maybe even a second family. For women the crisis is generally medically described, by the dreaded 'm-word' . . . menopause. For many women entering their sixth decade, it's an intense period of hormonal change that, unfortun-ately, often coincides with their mate's own problems. It's a recipe for marital disaster.

My case was fairly typical. I suffered the classic symptoms of needing to come to terms with the next stage of my life. My children had grown and left home, my parents were both dead and my husband was absorbed in his career, as he had been for our entire partnership. I needed to set a new direction; to find new challenges. I was indeed lost and more than a little frightened. But I was also excited and energised by the prospect of what might lie ahead for me.

Looking back with the smattering of wisdom I've gained over the past seven years, I realise what I was really looking for was passion. My life had been punctuated by periods of intense and passionate existence. My love of nature as a wild child growing free at the beach; the heartfelt political fervour of my teens; my first loves, powerful and transforming; the exquisite pleasure of my pregnancies and births; the joys and laughter of motherhood; the unexpected delight of a successful career; and the deep rewards of caring for an ageing parent.

I couldn't abide the idea that from now on everything in my life would gradually wind down. My career would fill the gap left by the children no longer at home; my grandchildren would fill the gap left by a partner no longer hungry for my body; the care of my garden would fill the gap of a daily routine devoid of spontaneity or surprises. I knew in my heart that it was not enough. That I craved excitement and adventure and that I wasn't about to let go without a putting up a fight. No doubt this probably has something to do with growing up as a baby boomer, a generation that particularly valued youth – its excitements, its hedonism, and its idealism.

My story is not very different from many women of my age. We have placed high expectations on ourselves in the belief that we could have it all. Career, relationships, children, travel, financial security and good health. In many ways we *have* had it all and now we find it difficult – if not impossible – to just let go. To surrender to ageing and, eventually, to death.

Yet we have no choice. We can have plastic surgery and work frenetically at the gym and even take human growth hormones to trick our bodies into thinking we are thirty-five, but at the end of the day we have to face the fact that our lives are gradually slowing down. This is not to say we can't still have fun, but we should also be looking for more than that. For understanding, for meaning and for a more deeply satisfying existence.

Looking back at those 'lost' years, I realise that despite the pain they contained, they were a vital part of my evolution as an older woman. I'm not for a moment suggesting that every woman should break out, fly to a foreign land and take a lover. It's a perilous adventure and one that can easily lead to disaster. Yet for me it was a reaction to a life spent working hard and putting the needs of others ahead of my own. It was my wild time, my lost youth, my compensation for not having explored my sexuality in my teens before I met David.

I also recognise that the woman I became during those rocky years was still me, it was just a different version of me that I hadn't acknowledged before. We all have many sides to our nature, some of which we repress for obvious reasons. I know, for example, that I consciously tried to be a totally different sort of parent to my own parents and yet, ultimately, I have to acknowledge now that certain patterns of behaviour crept through and affected my parenting style. I know now that while the persona I chose to present to my family and friends, and to the wider world, was the responsible, hard-working and giving side of my character (I refuse to use the term self-sacrificing because it smacks of martyrdom), there is another, darker side to me that's prepared to be selfish and self-indulgent. It's still there, I just have it more under control these days.

My life has changed significantly over the past four years and this, quite naturally, has had an effect on my decisions and priorities. My sister's decline into dementia, my grand-daughter's profound disabilities, my children's marriage breakdowns, my husband's health problems and my own confrontation with a potentially fatal disease have brought me back to earth with a big thud. Of course, I could have chosen to ignore these problems within my family and continued to enjoy my newfound sense of freedom. Yet that option never occurred to me. My instinctive response was to rearrange my life so that I could be as involved and supportive as possible. This isn't saintly, it's just plain commonsense. For more than thirty years the main focus of my life has been the nurture of my family, so why would I abandon them just when they needed me the most? It's not a change of heart; it's just an acceptance that this is what's essential for me at this period of my life.

All this has given me cause for deep reflection and self-examination. Not navel-gazing, but a shot at using the problems that have cropped up to help gain insight and understanding. It's not 'meaning of life' stuff; more a striving to crystallise how I really feel about these big issues. I spent a great deal of my life just living day-to-day, carefree and loving every minute of it. Now I allow myself some quiet thinking time, and I sense this is a natural part of the ageing process. Although

I'm not physically slowing down too much yet – I'm just as busy as I ever was – these days I use my head as much as my heart when I make decisions. Is this the coming of wisdom? Is this why we are told that growing old has its compensations – because as our bodies deteriorate our minds store the knowledge of a lifetime and we (finally) become wise? I'm not so sure about this. My youngest son, Ethan, aged twenty-eight, has a very old head on young shoulders. The same applies to his partner, Lynne. They always had plenty of commonsense but the advent of Isabella into their lives has brought them wisdom and insight beyond their years. They have had to consider the possibility they may still be caring for a disabled daughter when they are in their sixties, and may never have the chance, as I did, to escape from their responsibilities.

How do I really feel about ageing? To be totally honest, I dislike it intensely. I desperately try to think positively about it, but the downsides loom large. I don't equate ageing with dying. To me, they are two separate issues. Somehow death doesn't faze me quite as much as the actual ageing process. I see death as inevitable and not to be feared. I don't look forward to it, especially if I am unfortunate enough to experience a long, lingering and painful demise. But I accept it and believe that it's OK to die.

Yet I can't seem to be as philosophical about growing old. For me, the process is accompanied by a sense of loss. I'm no longer as strong as I once was. I don't have the vigour and the stamina to work endless hours in the garden or to haul large bags of grain around for the poultry. I can't carry children on my hip any more – it throws my back out and I end up hobbling around for week. This makes me wild because I have always loved having a child on my hip, especially when I'm cooking dinner. I can run but I'm not as confident climbing a tall ladder these days and my eyesight is failing to the point that I never know the shampoo from the conditioner in the shower. I can't even read a newspaper headline without my glasses. My skin has become dry and papery, no matter how much moisturiser I massage into it day and night. Quite frankly, my hair is also falling out. This may all seem trivial and vain, but I just can't help resenting it. David is eleven years further down the track than me and he doesn't like it any more than I do. His teeth are breaking off, one by one, as a result of poor dentistry in the 1940s and 50s. His late-onset diabetes means his hair is also disappearing – his luxuriant beard has thinned dramatically and even the hair on his legs and arms has fallen out. His back causes him problems and he creaks out of bed every morning, often muttering 'I'm so old, and I don't like it'.

Yet we both still have energy, we both work, we make love, we exercise and eat well and enjoy our lives. It's just that after fifty-five the ageing process seems to accelerate and while we have to accept it, we certainly don't have to say that we like it. I don't see us as a pair of whingers, complaining about minor ailments. I'm sure very many people feel exactly as we do, it's just that our society doesn't encourage us to say so.

Our relationship has been through so much over the past eight years and it's now stronger and more resilient than ever. I no longer dwell on my husband's negative attributes, nor simmer with resentment about his failings. He feels the same way about me. Perhaps that's one positive aspect of growing older. A growing acceptance and a greater tolerance. I'm very keen, however, not to allow our partnership to slip into complacency. I still like to surprise David; to keep him on his toes. The frisson is still there between us and I know that's partly because we managed to pull our marriage back from the brink. We no longer take each other for granted.

In an interview on ABC-TV, Woody Allen said he would rather trade the wisdom he has gained over the past thirty-five years and have those years back to live again. I don't feel quite that disturbed about growing older, but I do understand exactly where he's coming from. I applaud his bravery in admitting his dislike of growing old.

Ultimately I know I have a great deal to look forward to. My grandchildren sustain me with hope and optimism and I feel confident that I will live long enough to meet a great-grandchild or two. Even Isabella, with her ongoing problems, has such a grasp on life and a profound impact on our family that I cannot imagine the world without her. I hope that if I do live to be a grand age I will be a thoroughly impish and eccentric old woman with a sense of humour and a capacity for loving, laughing and having fun.

Christmas is coming round again, and this year I have a little more time for preparations. We've had a wet spring – even some snow in late November – and the garden here at the farm has never looked more beautiful. The bird life is prolific in this district, and as I write the bottlebrush outside my office window is filled with upside-down wattlebirds and honeyeaters feasting on the nectar. There are more snakes around this year too, and I've had several hair-raising close encounters. My vegetable garden is planted and I'm about to cut back the first flush of flowers on the roses. I feel contented.

Predictably, my life has recently become even more complicated. Both my children who separated have now found new partners, and so has my former son-in-law. I've met them all and warmed to them, and needless to say there are more children involved. When I add on my extra grandchildren, as I like to think of them, I'm now up to fourteen. All our extended family will come to stay at various times over the holiday period, including Miriam and her new partner, Mark, Lorna, and Rick and his partner, Shelley. My long dining table, designed for an expanding family, can no longer accommodate the entire *ménage* at one time. The children will have to be relegated to the other long table, on the verandah! I'm pleased that everything seems to be working out in the end. Through all the ups and downs we have remained close and the farm is still at the heart of it all.

AFTERWORD

When I'm not writing or gardening, or spending time with my grandchildren, or travelling around the world for work or to care for my sister, I spend time as a public speaker, which is a sideline I thoroughly enjoy.

It started back when I was first writing gardening books in the early 1980s. After the publication of my very first book I was approached by a local gardening club in the Mountains to be a guest speaker at their monthly meeting in the church hall. I was petrified at the thought. Although I had been a debater at school I had not stood up in front of an audience since that time.

For that first talk I made copious notes and in the end wrote a speech which I intended to read. I wasn't going to be caught out making any mistakes.

I surprised myself by not even glancing at my notes, let alone following my prepared lecture. I spoke off the cuff, made a few jokes and stimulated an easy question-and-answer session at the end. The hour flew, and the next time I was approached I did not have the same reservations.

Over the following fifteen years I cut my teeth as a public speaker, talking to gardeners in clubs all over Australia. I loved meeting people, and laughing about the eccentricities of keen gardeners. I loved the warm-hearted banter and exchanges that became an inevitable part of the public-speaking process.

More recently, I have talked to large groups each time a new book of mine has been published, and I have also set aside time to speak at events organised to raise funds for charity. It's extraordinary how a simple gathering – a morning tea or cocktail party with a guest speaker – can raise such large sums of money in just a few hours (although of course there's a lot work for the organisers in the lead-up to such an event).

Over the years, from my days as a gardening writer to my current role as the unofficial spokeswoman of middle-aged women yearning to run away from home, I have developed a great rapport with my readers and this always makes for a lively exchange of ideas and viewpoints. Keen readers love to meet authors and because I write in an honest way they really feel as though they know me, which is great. It means, of course, that it's no holds barred when it comes to question time and I sometimes reel at some of the questions I am asked on these occasions . . .

'How did your husband react,' one well-dressed woman enquired, 'when he realised you were having . . . an extra cup of coffee after dinner?'

Audience laughter. I knew what she was getting at.

'I don't drink coffee,' I think I quickly retorted. Then went on to answer her question more earnestly.

'Do you still see your lover?' asked another.

'Yes. But it's different now.'

'How did his wife feel?'

'She didn't know, thank heavens.'

And so it goes.

Inevitably I am asked if there will be another book in the series. People must love to hear other people's stories. There is a thirst for books that take people on a journey through the life of another. There are so many people who lead fascinating lives and we just can't seem to get enough of them.

The feedback I get through my website confirms this. Almost every day I am sent an email – sometimes two or three – from readers wanting to talk about my books. Their letters bubble with enthusiasm and they always ask . . . what happened next?

I picked up your book Au Revoir *at the library recently and I just wanted to tell you how much I enjoyed it . . . and I absolutely loved the funeral you gave your Mum . . . that was just the best!!!!!*
I look forward to reading more
Wendy

I know i'm a bit slow off the mark but i love your books and feel i know you and you make me feel normal at our age. In your writing you say it how it is warts and all. I've just realised you have the third book – the long hot summer. I can't wait to get my hands on it. Thank you once again, you are an inspiration to all us 50-something chooks. I like you don't want to get old because i'm really only 30. ha ha
regards judy

You are an amazing lady Mary! I have just finished reading The Long Hot Summer *following on from your previous two books and my head is still spinning thinking of all you have been through and how you have survived it all. You would be an inspiration to so many women. I hope to get to the NSW Art Gallery so I can hear you in person for the first time. Many blessings to you and don't ever stop being so honest and open.*

I've enjoyed getting lost in your books and would like to know what tours in France you may have during 2009. Thank you for such wonderfully descriptive stories, I certainly got lost in them – with a cheeky little glass of red in hand!

I am a huge fan and have enjoyed all three of your biographies (just finished The Long Hot Summer). *Fantastic, I felt everything with you throughout your journey . . . A devoted fan, Heather*

I have thoroughly enjoyed reading your books. I can relate so well being 49 myself and dedicating my life so far to my family, after reading *Au Revoir* I decided I needed to travel myself and find my old self. I have just returned from Europe which was wonderful but just a taste for the future.

I have finished *Last Tango in Toulouse* and am just starting *The Long Hot Summer*. I commend you on your honesty, and hope one day to find my way to the little part of the world you make sound so wonderful in your books. Keep the stories coming please.
Love Maree

I try to respond to most of the emails, although when I'm on the road it isn't always easy. However these messages encourage me enormously, and give me confidence to keep writing on subjects that are touchy for some people (especially male book reviewers).

In France, people now coming looking for my house. If I'm at home they sometimes knock on the door and say hello. I'm usually happy to see them, unless I'm in the middle of some domestic crisis, or right on deadline for a piece of writing. But it can be a little unsettling for me at times, because it's the last thing I expect when I'm in such a remote place as the tiny village of Frayssinet-le-Gelat. People leave notes for me at Jeannette and Sylvie's restaurant in Pomarede, and every time I return I am handed a small bundle of messages and cheerios, often written on paper napkins. Once, I was photographed unloading groceries from the boot of my car and carrying them into the house. The couple who took the pictures didn't approach me at the time but later mailed me a copy of one. I have to confess I found that a bit creepy.

I look forward to my next tour when I can talk at literary and fundraising events about the issues I have raised in this latest book. Naturally, my readers are still probably thinking of me as a free spirit, and it will be interesting to see how they react to the latest chapter in my story. Will they think I have hung up my fishnet tights in favour of pastimes more sedate and saintly?

I certainly hope not!

ACKNOWLEDGMENTS

Although writing is a solitary occupation, creating a finished book is a collaborative effort. During the writing of *Sweet Surrender* I was offered tremendous love and forbearance by my family, my friends and work colleagues. My husband supported my spending as much time as I could with my sister; my children and their families listened and laughed at my blunderings through mid-life. I am fortunate indeed that my agent Lyn Tranter has been such a staunch ally and that my compassionate publisher Tom Gilliatt no longer looks alarmed at *anything* I tell him. Sybil Nolan, as editor, found the storyline amid the confusion and was later capably backed up by Pan Macmillan senior editor Emma Rafferty and copy editor Ali Lavau. The typesetters, proofreader, cover designer, publishing assistants and publicists — a huge thank you to everyone involved.